cool hotels

Kim Inglis

photography by
Jacob Termansen and Pia Marie Molbech

PERIPLUS

contents

The New Asian Hotel: A Sanctuary for the Senses

Recent years have seen an Asian design boom, with Oriental-influenced spas, architecture, interior design, furnishings and handicrafts gaining recognition in the world arena. Global attention is focused on the East—for inspiration, ideas and aesthetics—and increasingly as a holiday destination.

India, Sri Lanka and the Maldives have always been visited, but it is only in the last decade or so that they have begun to build ground-breaking, internationally acclaimed hotels, villas and resorts. In this book we showcase what we consider to be the best the region has to offer. Often trendy, and definitely seductive, jaw-droppingly beautiful, knock-your-socks-off stunning, sometimes modern minimalist, other times simply stylish, each property is unique. There are chic urban resting holes, modish rustic retreats, sybaritic sea-sand-and-sun resorts, even a private island or two. Places to escape to, to surrender to the power of pure visual artistry—and chill. Places where your soul will be soothed and your senses seduced. Places where high-style hedonism has been elevated to an art form.

Until reasonably recently, cultural tourists to the area would have restricted their visits to the Delhi-Agra-Jaipur triangle and the kaftan-and-kiff set would have settled for a beach in Goa, Sri Lanka or possibly the Maldives. But with better transport links, a more demanding clientele and some stunning off-the-tourist-track properties, the scene is changing. Be it the joy of the remote, the thrill of the city, a beach, jungle or mountain location, or a combination of the above, the region delivers. And in environments that are design-worthy and intelligent.

Individuality is key. Some hotels are incredibly simple (one even has no electricity, phone or running water), others are swanky, six-star and super-deluxe. At some there's an eco-friendly ethos, at others the emphasis is on heritage and history. There are city-slick modernist cubes, home-away-from-home hostelries, hip hideaways and renovated forts and palaces. Some are recognized brands, others are privately owned and run. Many are recently opened, representing a new wave of consumer-led hotel architecture that offers peace, privacy and escape in drop-dead gorgeous surroundings.

All the hotels in this book dare to be different. Visually, architecturally and in terms of size, location and amenities, they vary widely; where they are similar is in their commitment to quality. They are also ravishingly photogenic. Enjoy.

The Imperial New Delhi, India

For those who know India well, it is somehow comforting to arrive in Delhi, see a cow nonchalantly walking in the middle of the road, note the mayhem of traffic, and reminisce about the noise, confusion and Indian-ness of it all. For first-timers, however, it can be a little overwhelming. The smells, the barrage of humanity, the honking of horns—all interesting, different, but somehow too much.

This is only one of the reasons why I recommend the Imperial as the hotel of choice in Delhi: for a start, a black Tata Safari or a swanky Mercedes S320 with leather upholstery (instead of an ancient Ambassador that makes a noise rather like a sewing machine on speed) picks you up from the airport, the driver is wonderfully welcoming and informative, pointing out buildings of interest along the way, and the oasis of quiet and calm offered at the entrance gate to the hotel alleviates any worries. Check-in is efficient and friendly and on arrival at the room, all is ordered, beautiful and comforting.

Other reasons are too numerous to list: the art deco structure is in an architectural league of its own, the hotel has just completed an enormous restoration that has transformed its interiors, its historical legacy is legendary, there are over 4,000 original artworks within its walls, the be-turbanned or besuited staff outnumber guests by a 3-to-1 ratio, and proudly adhere to that phrase describing Indian hospitality, "*Athithi Devo Bhava*" or "Guest is God." Furthermore, it is the only hotel in India to have been selected as a member of Preferred Hotels & Resorts Worldwide, a global brand of 110 of the world's finest and most distinctive independently owned luxury hotels and resorts. One word sums up the Imperial: impressive. Make that two: very impressive.

Designed and built in 1931 by DJ Bromfield, an associate of Sir Edwin Lutyens, the Imperial was inaugurated by Lord Willingdon in 1933. Lutyens envisaged that it would be the most luxurious hotel in New Delhi, located as it was on the prestigious Queensway (now Janpath), with a unique blend of Victorian, colonial and informal art deco. Sure enough, its pillared verandahs, 8 acres (3.2 hectares) of sprawling gardens, dining rooms, tea lounges and Royal Ballroom soon became the

places to see and be seen. Guests from abroad marveled at its high-domed atrium, marble floors and art deco wall panels, not to mention the elegantly appointed rooms and suites. More significantly, it was within the precincts of the Imperial that Jawaharlal Nehru, Rajendra Prasad and Dr Radhakrishnan held talks about the integration of the princely states into the Union of India and Mohammed Ali Jinnah and Nehru discussed the formation of modern-day Pakistan.

The Imperial recently underwent a major renovation and restoration process under the aegis of Hong Kong-based architect Chandu Chhada. Unlike other so-called heritage hotels where the reworking has resulted in a sanitized, specious recreation of the original, the Imperial has emerged with its original atmosphere intact and all the benefits of modern technology on tap. Its historical legacy—be it in the gold deco design motifs on the lifts echoed on the stone in the ballroom, the superb collection of lithographs, paintings and photographs depicting the British presence in the subcontinent and the landscapes and peoples of India itself, or the meticulously restored period furniture—speaks volumes about the past. But backward-looking it is not. Set firmly in the present are the lines ensuring instant internet connection in all the rooms, the minimalist flower-and-candle arrangements in the corridors, the new music in the public areas (watch out for the Imperial CD), the Bang & Olufsen TV sets in the deco wing and a 100 percent commitment to innovation.

Even though the Imperial describes itself as a "museum hotel," it never seems stuffy or stilted. Rather, it encourages interaction between guest and artwork: you feel comfortable lingering in front of a panoramic photograph of the Coronation Durbar, or if you wander into the Royal Ballroom, you're invited in to admire the magnificent fresco by Bourne & Shepherd that lines the wall atop the stairs. You can take a history tour of the hotel with Ominder Singh Chaudhury, the resident curator who is cataloguing the giant art collection. Or you can just chat with any member of staff who happens to be passing. Staff in the Patiala Peg, the cosy 28-seat bar lined with a remarkable set of photographs of the maharajah of Patiala during World War II, are only too happy to tell you the story of how their bar got its name. Fable has it that the maharajah's team beat the viceroy's at a tent-pegging competition. By plying the opposing team's players with pegs of whisky much larger than the usual ones the night before, and by giving them smaller tent pegs during the match itself, they ensured the maharajah's victory. Giving a nod to history, the bar celebrates the tale by serving 75-milliliter shots instead of the usual 60 milliliters.

Such stories give a human frame to what is essentially a monumental structure, and explain, in large part, why the Imperial is as popular today as it was in the past.

1 Janpath, New Delhi 110 001, India
tel: +91 11 2334 1234   fax: +91 11 2334 2255
email: luxury@theimperialindia.com   www.theimperialindia.com

The Manor   New Delhi, India

Hoardings in bright colors declaring "Aarti Plastic House," "Casuals and Formals," "Don't be in the Dark: Ecopower" line the road. There is heat, concrete and dust; a tsunami of fruit sellers, rickshaw-*wallahs* and drivers with their hands super-glued to their horns, hordes of beggars and cripples. Delhi seems especially confusing and confrontational. My driver has Bollywood movie-music blaring at full volume—and I can't banish terrifying visions of a head-on collision. It is serious sensory overload time. I want to turn the Indian tap off, and switch channels to "normal."

Enter the Manor. An oasis of cool in a cacophonous city. So cool that it isn't in any guidebook. So cool you have to direct the taxi driver to the exclusive gated residential suburb where it is located. The hotel's only downside is that it is a little off the beaten track—45 minutes drive from the airport and 30 minutes from the station. But no matter, once you head into the exclusive suburb of Friends Colony, you know you've arrived. Here, lawns seem the size of football pitches, the streets have speed bumps, and you can hear birds singing. Cross the threshold of Number 77…and exhale.

All is clean, spare and contemporary. Aggressive air-conditioning, sleek lines and angles, the cool of slate and tile, smooth terrazzo floors and a bevy of boys attending to luggage and ushering me into the lobby. An efficient check-in, an ice-cold drink, and the calm of a room in soothing colors where sound-proofing really works. Then a shower with hot water from the tap… Bliss.

It seems horribly ungenerous when in India to want something non-Indian. But, occasionally, you need a fix—and the Manor provides it. Once you're past the woven copper gates, and onto the cobbled stone drive inset with river stones, you could be anywhere. That is its greatest asset. There is a wonderful western menu at the slick restaurant Seventy Seven; or you can have Indian dishes if you prefer. The staff is rigorous, helpful and all speak excellent English; they could have been trained at the Four Seasons. There is instant internet connectivity in each room and the hotel thoughtfully provides you with a laptop if you don't have one. You want a cheese sandwich at 3 am? No problem, there is 24-hour room service.

So how did this 18-room gem of a hotel come about? Housed in a two-storey 1950s country house with generous rooms and bathrooms, terraces and a verandah overlooking an extensive lawn, the building was originally on the outskirts of Delhi. As the suburbs encroached, it became part of the city. In 1998 husband-and-wife team Vinay Kapoor and Shirley Fujikawa of London's Studio u+a decided to transform it into Delhi's first boutique hotel (Kapoor is one of the co-owners). It was an idea ahead of its time, especially in India—but the gamble paid off. People have taken to the concept surprisingly well, and the hotel is often full. It is sensible to book in advance.

"The Studio u+a design team believes in creating environments where the whole is always greater than the sum of its parts," explains Fujikawa. "Our approach at the Manor was to minimize the distinction between landscape, architectural design and interiors and create an environment where each forms a part of an integrated whole." Working with a local project manager to renovate the building completely, Studio u+a aimed for a contemporary design that didn't neglect classic comfort. "A terrazzo firm in Milan custom made the floors to our design," says Fujikawa, "while the carpets were woven in India to our specifications. What made this project so challenging was the fact that everything had to be designed—furniture, accessories, floral displays, graphics, even uniforms! In the end, the concept succeeds only if the details reinforce the concept."

The overall aim was to create a timeless feel, and this the Manor certainly has. It's the sort of place that will still look great a decade or more from now. Public spaces are characterized by geometric forms and wonderfully tactile materials: a slate wall lies adjacent to a backlit onyx panel, and wooden paneling offers a sensory contrast. The color scheme follows on into the adjacent public bathrooms where dramatically patterned yellow travertine slabs create some of the best loos I've had occasion to use. Mosaic and terrazzo floors and custom-made furniture accentuate the cool, sharp look. This is carried on into the rooms and bathrooms, where high-quality materials are married with simple, sleek lines. Luxurious silk curtains, custom-designed wood, upholstered furniture and hand-knotted carpets are in natural tones with black accents. Bathrooms feature huge slabs of deep green granite, mirrored surfaces and lighter green stone walls and floors.

Everything works at the Manor, both design-wise and in reality. In a country like India, where the unexpected is often the norm, this is a rare treat. And a final plus-point: tipping is taboo.

77 Friends Colony (West), New Delhi 110 065, India
tel: +91 11 2692 5151   fax: +91 11 2692 2299
email: manordel@ndf.vsnl.net.in   www.themanordelhi.com

Amarvilas Agra, India

Try to arrive at Amarvilas at dusk, as that is when the hotel is at its most magical. You'll definitely hear a muezzin calling the faithful in the distance, his plaintive tones rising, falling and echoing off the stone walls; there will probably be the harsh cry of a peacock too, and the silhouettes of crows wheeling overhead. Walk up the steps, past two stone sentinel elephants—and prepare to be amazed. In front of you is an astoundingly lit colonnaded forecourt or *bidadari* (*see previous pages),* complete with blazing torches or *mashals*, 64 carved stone fountains, reflecting pools, and scalloped-edged Rajasthani-style arched cloisters lined with Mughal-style inlay and gold leaf stenciling. It's like a scene from *The Arabian Nights* meeting the velvet Indian sky.

Then it is only a short walk through a domed reception area (*overleaf*) in gold leaf and cobalt blue to any number of views of the Taj Mahal. Amarvilas, one of the prestigious Oberoi "vilas" properties, is situated only 600 meters (2,000 feet) from this most delicate of monuments, and offers magnificent vistas of it at every turn. Floor-to-ceiling windows from lounges, bars, restaurants, even some of the spa suites, give guests un-paralleled access to its creamy translucence. Take a lift up to any of the 105 rooms and suites, and view it from a different angle from your own private terrace. The appearance of the hotel seems to change almost hourly with subtle nuances in light and sky, and you could almost be forgiven for not wanting to spoil it by going close up.

It is said that an estimated 20,000 skilled craftsmen labored for 22 years to build the Taj Mahal. At Amarvilas, it was eight years from conception to completion, with a full four years dedicated to the work that needed to be done by 600 Oberoi artisans. Even though the architecture borrows from Turkish, Rajput and Moorish traditions, as well as Mughal ones, the materials and meticulous workmanship take their cue from Shah Jehan and his team.

Red Samathra sandstone and pure white Thassos marble (harder and less prone to marking than the Taj's Makrana quarried marble) are the predominant materials; they echo the red-and-white combination so favored by the Mughals. Italian Satvario marble with dark veins is employed as flooring, and beige Karoli stone from Rajasthan is also widely used. The geometric patterning of the two colors was inspired by similar use in earlier forts and palaces—and it is interesting to note that for the most part these surfaces are left unblemished—allowing the stone to speak for itself. There's an austerity both inside and outside, with only a few choice artifacts, one or two floral arrangements and no indoor plants and potted plants elsewhere. This allows the impeccable craftsmanship to take center stage.

And this is truly magnificent. There are examples of the *pachikari* inlay favored by the Mughals, whereby minute slivers of precious and semi-precious stones—such as green nephrite jade, lapis lazuli, amber, turquoise and malachite—are set in complex stylized floral designs into a marble base. Like the Taj with its filigree screens in the tomb area, Amarvilas has similar screens with *jaali* patterns (*jaali* means "net" or "mesh" in Urdu). The Mughals were great naturalists; the Persian poet Abu Talib Kalim was so enthused by the inlay work on monuments commissioned by Shah

Jehan that he wrote in a poem: "They have inlaid stone flowers in marble/which surpass reality in color if not in fragrance." At Amarvilas, delicate floral patterns in gold leaf are applied on various walls.

Outside, by the lapis-colored, mosaic-lined pool there is a fabulous gold Ganesh painted against an azure wall. Across the water is a colonnaded terrace, with more painstakingly applied gold leaf floral patterning. On either side, terraced water gardens rise from the central swimming pool where oversized tasseled umbrellas from Bali give the pool beds shade. With the ever-present sounds of gurgling water and the backdrop of Mahal and mosaic, one could easily imagine oneself in some Mughal pleasure pavilion of old.

Despite the use of age-old techniques, there is a "here-and-now" feeling to the hotel that sets it firmly in 21st century India. Internet ports in the rooms, waste recycling and "green" practices in the household management—including the use of minimal-pollution propane gas—are only some of its futuristic features. Similarly, Amarvilas suits both young and old; traditionalists and trendsetters alike are attracted by its timeless style. Past guests have included Greek shipping magnates, sheiks from the Middle East and Moroccan princesses, as well as Indian film stars and movie moguls. It's entirely appropriate that its name translates as "Eternal Abode": amar is "eternal," vilas translates as "resting place" or "abode."

Taj East Gate Road, Taj Nagri Scheme, Agra 282 001, India
tel: +91 562 231515   fax: +91 562 231516
email: reservations@oberoi-amarvilas.com   www.oberoihotels.com

Take the aggravation out of Agra and check into Amarvilas. Throughout the hotel, cobalt blue, gold and the patina of Burma teak floors are offset by austere stone, marble and sumptuous drapes, carpets and upholstery. Kashmiri embroidery works well with cotton *rasais* (quilts) in the rooms, while flashes of kingfisher blue are seen in the lampshades and soft furnishings. Named after India's most famous diamond, the Kohinoor Suite (*opposite below*) is the most exclusive. Here antiques, such as an ebony and ivory-inlay armoire, match modern custom-made pieces seamlessly.

ITC Hotel Sonar Bangla Sheraton & Towers   Kolkata, India

We've got eco-resorts, business hotels, country retreats, hip urban resting places—you name it.
What once was the humble hotel is now a huge hospitality industry, with a hundred different niche
markets. So when I was told about a "business resort" in Kolkata (Calcutta) that had opened on
New Year's Eve of 2002, I didn't bat an eyelid at the term. After all, people have always combined
business with pleasure, haven't they?

Yes, but perhaps not in quite such spectacular style. For the Sonar Bangla Sheraton & Towers,
the latest offering from that mega-giant of Indian hoteliering, ITC Hotels Ltd, caters to both business-
person and tourist in a state-of-the-art kind of way. Set over 16 acres (6.5 hectares) of land roughly
half-way between the city center and the airport, the hotel is an awesome construction. First
impressions are of dramatic high ceilings, natural light filtering in from all sides, long internal views
and water everywhere; there's a minimal design ethos that never seems empty or sterile. Quite
the opposite in fact. As all the rooms, both public and private, are huge, there is a wonderfully
spacious, airy feeling throughout—clean and deceptively simple, with a mix of quality artworks,
luxurious furniture and small, carefully chosen design pieces.

ITC prides itself on pioneering the concept of "the hotel within a hotel" and at Sonar Bangla,
all public spaces are contained within one block, while the rooms are housed separately. This is
an inspired idea: the atmosphere in the dramatic, high-ceilinged lobby or in the lounges, bars and
restaurants—areas which form the activity hub of the hotel—is buzzy and informal, with a type of
European or American luxury pervading throughout. But walk across the lawns or waterways to
one of the residential blocks, and immediately all is quiet, calm and serene. Giving the buildings a
sense of connection and cohesion is an impressive 120-meter (400-foot) watercourse (*right and
below*) that runs the full length of the hotel—apparently the largest in any hotel in India. Courtyards
and colonnades provide breathing space, while brick or wooden screens allow for the dramatic
throw of shadow and light.

The rooms (*overleaf*) are sexy, soft and very easy on the eye. You feel pampered as soon as the door clicks behind you, as there is space and light everywhere, fabrics are luxurious, tones are restful and mod-cons plentiful. Whether you've endured a day of meetings or enjoyed time out at the spa, they are welcoming and super-comfortable. There's a massage chair to soothe sore muscles, huge flatscreen TV and (in some of the higher-end rooms) a giant TV at the end of the tub. If you are watching television and the phone rings, as soon as you pick up the receiver, the volume on the TV turns to mute. Very New York, I thought.

Other thoughtful touches include Japanese fan coil units for silent air cooling, blackout curtains (a boon for the jetlagged) and glass screens separating the bathroom from the living/bedroom. Such are the gizmos of the hotel. The nuts and bolts are equally impressive. There's a chip-and-putt golf course, a massive spa, near Olympic-length swimming pool, tennis courts, jogging track, bars, lounges, seven restaurants and fully digitalized business facilities. Service is efficient, but kind too. And everywhere you go, the design is city-slick and cool.

Singapore-based architect Kerry Hill was the creative force behind the Sonar Bangla. In much of his work, context provides the focus for content, and the Sonar Bangla is no exception. "We took inspiration from the louvers, trellises and shutters in Calcutta's architecture whilst formulating the hotel," he says. "And also the rivers and surrounding water bodies. In the beginning, there was quite a division of ideas between the client and myself, but over the five years it took to plan and construct the hotel, we came closer and closer together. By the end, we were in agreement on most things; I believe ITC is happy with the result."

"Absolutely," confirms general manager, Ranvir Bhandari, "We have created a product that truly reflects the spirit of Bengal." Bhandari points out that many have compared the hotel to the quintessential *baganbaari* or riverside country house of Bengal's landowners of old. Although there is clearly a lapse of scale in such a comparison, there is a connection to place throughout. For example, art consultant Ina Puri selected a varied and exciting collection of paintings by both old and young artists from Calcutta to grace the hotel's walls and the huge statues in the lobby are copies from Calcutta's Indian Museum. Horticulturalist Suhash Joshi based the landscaping around the plants of east India, collecting many rare specimens and types of bamboo to accompany the water features. And on the culinary front, Master Chef Imtiaz Quereshi, whose ancestors set up the famous Royal Hotel in Calcutta decades ago, has dug out recipes from memory to make sure authentic Bengali food is served in some of the seven restaurants.

Sonar Bangla has a strong modernity that allows it to look to the future whilst still paying homage to the past. It prides itself as a showcase for Bengal and is giving its all to live up to its name (*sonar* translates as "golden"). Does it exemplify the Indian hotel of the future? Watch this space.

1 JBS Halden Avenue, Opp Science City, Kolkata 700 046, India
tel: +91 33 2345 4545   fax: +91 33 2345 4455
email: mail@welcomgroup.com   www.welcomgroup.com

Ananda—in the Himalayas Tehri Garhwal, India

Ananda hovers, as if in a bubble, high in the Himalayas overlooking the eternal Mother Ganga and the pilgrimage site of Rishikesh. On a clear day you can see the mighty river and the small ashram town far below, but when the cloud comes into the valley, the only sight is of the pristine ochre Ananda buildings bathed in sunlight and caressed with rarefied air. Isolated and serene, it pulses with an energy, yet soothes with quiet and cool. One guest described it as "almost surreal," straddling as it does both the real world (rooms, restaurant, spa) and the ethereal (maharajah's palaces, holy sages, forested mountains, and clear, pollution-free mountain air).

The Ananda experience begins at Haridwar Railway Station or Dehra Dun Airport, where you are picked up by chauffeured jeep. A cassette tape playing devotional music interspersed with information about the resort sets the tone. Crossing the River Ganges, the jeep begins the climb up some 1,000 meters (1,200 yards) through forested hillside to the 100-acre (40-hectare) estate of the maharajah of Tehri-Garhwal. Vultures on blasted trees stare unblinking out to air, eagles lazily circle on the thermals and ubiquitous monkeys scamper from tree to tree. The dense *sal* forest is home to tigers as well, I'm told.

Crested gates swing open when you reach the top; past the façade of the maharajah's original 19th century palace (*right*) and on to the Viceregal Lodge he built in 1911 as a guesthouse for the British viceroy (a visit that ironically never occurred). This is the Ananda reception, where all is orderly, calm and soothing. A duo of musicians flanked by Bijapuri arches play on the terrace, and the reception hall where you check in is resplendent with ancestral portraits, black-and-white photographs of past British rulers, including ones signed by Queen Elizabeth II in 1937 and Lord and Lady Mountbatten, art deco furniture, drapes and Venetian crystal chandeliers. The welcome is genuine.

Formalities over, it is from here a short buggy ride along a ridge past the music pavilion, sunset viewing point, squash court, mini golf course and spa to the residential block. A modern structure, it is built over five floors and hugs the edge of the promontory, seeming to float above the valley in a series of tiered steps. Each luxurious room has a balcony—with views either over the valley or back to the maharajah's palace, which looks especially dramatic when lit up at night.

Even though Ananda describes itself as a lifestyle destination spa—which it certainly is—this is definitely no pain-is-gain, bread-and-water retreat. In fact, it is luxurious in many senses of the word. You can choose to partake as little or as much as you like in the various health, relaxation and rejuvenation programs on offer. In addition to Ayurvedic and Western therapies, there is yoga, meditation, hydrotherapy and a fully equipped gymnasium and lap pool, with resident nurse, Ayurvedic doctor and physiotherapist on hand. The best spa therapists are probably those trained in Asia; not only are they intuitive, knowledgeable and loving, they radiate inner goodness. It is easy to surrender to their healing hands. They make you feel special, and if serenity, soul-soothing and stress-busting are on your agenda, Ananda delivers—big time.

Ananda ("bliss and contentment" in Sanskrit) is not new to healing and devotion. The maharajah of Garhwal, a pious person himself, invited renowned spiritual leader Ma Anandamayi to set up a base at his palace, and it was from here that she established her ashram propagating universal love and brotherhood, and became a respected figure in India. The legacy of Ma Anandamayi's all-pervading love eases throughout the entire resort: in the same way that the scent of roses—from the flower petals in the room, the rose-tinted spectacles I was wearing, the scented body lotion in the bathroom—wafted through my stay like a blessing, so did this feeling of warmth and love.

It took me precisely half an hour to settle into the rhythms of Ananda. The days began with an early morning yoga session or invigorating jog; followed by fresh fruit and baked delicacies on the Tree Tops deck. Then the only decision to be made was whether to have a swim, steam or sauna, relax on the balcony, or have one of the too-numerous-to-mention pampering treatments.

More often than not, the latter won through, but for those less self-indulgent, there is a vast range of activities. These include visits to the *aarti* at Rishikesh (the evening ritual where song and prayer are accompanied by releasing little "boats" of flowers and candles along the Ganges), white-water rafting and trips to the nearby Rajaji elephant wildlife reserve. Another delightful option—and many simply follow this route—is to simply unwind and relax. There's no better place for it.

The Palace Estate, Narendra Nagar, Tehri Garhwal, Uttaranchal 249 175, India
tel: +91 1378 227500   fax: +91 1378 227550
email: anandaspa@vsnl.com   www.anandaspa.com

The spa at the Ananda is refreshingly modern, with a reassuring no-nonsense air of professionalism.
That doesn't mean to say that it isn't beautiful too. With one floor for men and another for women,
it's a cool combination of green marble, sandstone and granite, interspersed with small internal courtyards with fountains. There is a separate Ayurvedic wing, each room containing a beautiful therapy
bed hand-crafted in Kerala from a single piece of *neem* wood. The relaxation areas and many of
the treatment rooms have dramatic views over the Himalayan landscape, as do many of the rooms.
Here, elegant touches include rose petals and lantana flowers floating in a copper bowl, stationery
folders in hessian and leather, recurring lotus images and individual private balconies. The Viceregal
Suite in the palace annexe is the most opulent of the resort's suites.

Neemrana Fort Palace   Alwar district, India

Is there such a thing as the "real Indian experience?" Perhaps it's easier to approach this question by listing what it is not. The "real India" is definitely not bug-infested backpackers' lodges and third-class rail travel; it also isn't the five-star luxury of new, opulent resorts (although we like some of these very much). Rather, it is a stay at some place like the Neemrana Fort Palace, an extraordinary heritage hotel that combines history and architectural grandeur with honest hospitality. I'd say a weekend there is about as authentic an Indian experience as you'll get anywhere on the subcontinent.

This is not to denigrate its more expensive, super-deluxe counterparts, some of which are featured in this book. If we're honest, those kinds of hotels lure us with a fantasy element; they take us to another world where we can forget our "real" lives and identities and become anyone we want. They're treats, they're pampering—and they're fun.

But somehow they don't seem real. Neemrana, on the other hand, is raw and real, the genuine article. Dating from the 15th century, and built in stages over 500 years, it is sited on a majestic plateau in the ancient Aravalli ranges. Whilst researching a book on Shekavati in the late '70s, owners Aman Nath and Francis Wacziarg first saw Neemrana glowing on a hill at sunset. It was subsequently bought in 1986 along with two partner-friends. Soon after the first wing was restored to open as a hotel in 1991, they asked their price to bow out, and today it is the flagship property of the Neemrana Group's hotels.

When work began, Neemrana's walls were crumbling, roofs had fallen in, and because nobody had lived there since 1947, villagers had pretty much looted all they could carry through its massive fortified doors. In fact, the doors themselves were about the only things they left behind—and that is because they were simply too heavy to shift! But gradually, over the years, the hotel took shape, and today, the fort palace boasts 42 rooms and suites, all different, all highly individual, situated in various nooks and crannies over nine levels.

As you progress ever upward, India in all its many facets is presented to you. Each room is named after an aspect of Indian life, or a region of the country. The Malabar Mahal sports woodwork from Kerala: part of a catamaran from the Malabar coast hangs from the ceiling and wood carvings taken from *nalakettu* or traditional warrior's homes are used both as interior and exterior decoration. Many others feature soft *chhapai* or block-printed cloth, that is hand-made locally. The queen's chambers, renamed the Sheesh Mahal or Hall of Mirrors after the original cut-glass ceiling, is resplendent in blue and white: colored glass on the windows, floaty white drapes, and the original geometric latticed windows or *jaalis* overlooking a central courtyard have been retained. Today, as in the past, you can see the goings on outside, but those outside cannot see in. One of the hotel restaurants, with scalloped-edged arches splitting the space into intimate areas, is dedicated to Raja Rajinder Singh, the last maharajah of Neemrana: old black-and-white family photographs and portraits grace the walls, and there's a sketch of his widow's house, the Vijay

Bagh, on the outskirts of the village. If you look closely, you can spot her modest home through the window; she, in turn, can see her former family seat from her terrace.

Like any traditional Indian dwelling, Neemrana revolves around a series of courts. Most are landscaped to some extent, and they lend the rambling palace some breathing space. But it's the exuberant collection of Indian art and artifacts that is particularly noteworthy; everywhere you turn, you are greeted by a statue, or an unusual piece of furniture or an object d'art. One semi-open hall, the Hindla Mahal (from hindola meaning "swing"), is dedicated solely to showcasing a selection of old Indian swings—from a colonial rocking cradle to some enormous examples from Gujarat, Rajasthan and South India. One gets the impression that a truck may just show up at any given moment, and disgorge a veritable treasure trove of paraphernalia personally collected by the owners.

By the millennium, the old palace was totally renovated. You'd have thought this would be the time for the owners to sit back and enjoy their creation. Right? "Actually, no," says Nath. "It was the time to expand. Neemrana has grown organically since 1464, and we are continuing the tradition." A new wing was added. In keeping with the monumental architecture, it houses a swimming pool made from stone crumbled from the billion-year-old hill, a gym, yoga room and Ayurvedic center below, an amphitheater for performances, and a conference center, museum and art gallery in Ghelot stone, so named after the nearby village where it is quarried. "But the whole palace is a gallery," I protested. "Yes, but there's always room for more," came the answer.

In 2001 the hotel earned the prestigious INTACH-SATTE award for Restoration and Tourism, and has now become synonymous with the phrase "restoration for reuse." As the judges noted: "Neemrana remains the foremost example of how we can pick architectural treasures from the national dustbin and turn them around into mainstream revenue earners in tourism."

Neemrana's proximity to Delhi, its indefatigable owners, and the new facilities it offers ensure a steady stream of visitors to this fairy-tale fortress. After more than half a century of neglect, Neemrana's mighty profile is once again cast against the Rajasthani horizon—a testament to vision, talent and sheer hard work.

Village Neemrana, District Alwar 301 030, Rajasthan, India
tel: +91 1494 46007   fax: +91 1494 46005
email: sales@neemranahotels.com   www.neemranahotels.com

Vanyavilas near Ranthambhore, India

The vast wooded estates of Indian princes used to teem with wildlife. Picnics and hunting trips were *de rigueur* for royalty, and many of their old hunting grounds are dotted with lakes, lodges and pleasure pavilions. What is today's Ranthambhore National Park was, from the turn of the century, the private hunting reserve of Jaipur's maharajahs, although it had been ruled locally, as the thousand-year-old fort atop its central hill testifies. But with control passing to Jaipur, the forests were closed to the public and stocked with birds and wildlife for *shikars*, or hunting expeditions.

On such occasions, a vast retinue of princes, kings, guests, hangers-on, servants, beaters as well as gun-bearers would have made the trip from the city to set up a home-away-from-home in a lakeside encampment. Typically these would have been tented, and in addition to kitchens, stables and sleeping chambers, there were pavilions for entertaining, dining and dancing. Royal tents were complex cloth palaces: inner layers were sumptuously embroidered and decorated, and came with fabric arches and different "rooms" for different functions. Gold and silver threads, velvets and silks, soft cushions and curtains adorned the interiors, while outer awnings constituted public areas. In many ways, such camps were portable recreations of court life.

Nowadays, visitors to Ranthambhore eschew hunting and shooting in favor of animal and bird watching. The park has had success in tiger preservation, and its ridges, lakes, woods and valleys are home to numerous species of deer, a rich variety of resident and migratory birds, hyenas, bears and jackals as well as a few leopards, coucals and over 30 resident tigers. Visits to the park are strictly monitored to avoid disruption to wildlife, and tiger sitings are quite frequent. Many visitors opt to stay in the semi-modernized royal lodge, but my recommendation is to check out Vanyavilas, a tented resort adjacent to the park. With a backdrop of the Aravalli cliffs and a meandering water garden setting, it is reminiscent of the old encampments of Rajput royalty.

Vanyavilas has an intimacy that is lacking at the other "vilas" properties. Set in a 22-acre (9-hectare) mango, lime and guava grove, it is super-deluxe (of course), but somehow smaller in

scale and temperament. All accommodation is in air-conditioned tents (ten twins and 15 doubles), although they are so luxurious you can hardly call them that. Each has a teak floor and proper walls, an outer canvas sheet that provides additional protection from wind and rain, and a softer inner layer beautifully embroidered with miniature tigers and floral motifs. Beds are four-poster or twin and there are the usual wonderful amenities we have come to expect from these properties. The bathroom has a claw-foot stand-alone tub, folding table and rolled up towels, giving the impression of transportability. It is as if the bathroom had just been set up for the night's camping, and could be dismantled and taken to the next camp the following day.

The public areas are set in a single-storey main building fashioned in the style of a traditional *haveli* or nobleman's home. From the ceremonial gatehouse, you walk past a modernist oblong water feature in Jaipur tiles of deep blue, to a teak door with brass inlay flanked by two elephant statues and flaming braziers. The severity of the entrance is softened by a reception lobby that sports frolicking elephants in gold leaf chasing each other around the ceiling architrave. All is fresh, open and cool. There's a snug colonial-style library, and access to a sweet-smelling courtyard where a *neem* tree would burst seasonally into lacelike flowers, scenting the air. Here a small pool flanked by tasseled parasols offers cool from the raging Rajasthani heat.

Because the focus of the resort is on the national park, conversations at dinner invariably center around who spotted which tiger and who trekked where. Choose between the indoor dining room where exuberant frescoes depict local scenes (*left*) and the sunken outdoor dining space. Seating is on the perimeter on stone benches; here Rajasthani appliqué cushions are arranged around a central fireplace that boasts a roaring log fire from December to March. The walls sport murals of trees in a homespun blue dye on a white background and two musicians in the corner play plaintive *ghazals* during your meal. Periwinkle blue ceramic plates enhance the summertime picnic feeling.

Members of staff are erudite and warm, and all speak excellent English. Nightly presentations by Fateh Singh Rathore, who for more than 25 years has been a resident of Ranthambhore, are lively and informative. Vanyavilas is lucky to have him as their resident naturalist. As Geoffrey C Ward writes in his book *Tiger-Wallahs* (2002): "Fateh has lived within Ranthambhore's forested heart as a ranger, mapped and built its roads as a wildlife warden, successfully shifted 12 villages from it as a field director, nearly lost his life defending it against outsiders intent upon its destruction, and helped to document for the first time the secret lives of tigers whose astounding openness his efforts made possible."

If you aren't hooked on tigers before you get to Vanyavilas, my bet is you will be by the time you leave. Those cuddly stripes are super-seductive.

Ranthambhore Road, Sawai Madhopur, Rajasthan 322 001, India
tel: +91 7462 223999   fax: +91 7462 223988
email: reservations@oberoi-vanyavilas.com   www.oberoihotels.com

Samode Palace near Jaipur, India

"Hurry, hurry…you're late," he hissed, then grabbed me by the arm and disappeared into the dark. I ran after him, through the courtyard, down the steps, through the next courtyard, the dark, heavy Rajasthani air like a blanket, and out through the front door ("two steps, mind"). Then I heard the distant music, and as my eyes adjusted to the darkness—I focused on the form of trees, four camels, two horses in the outer court, torches blazing and the fort lit up atop the hill. It was a traditional Rajasthani, red-carpet welcome for a group of visiting dignitaries. I'd almost missed it.

We only just had time to draw breath—and the group came through the main gate into the courtyard. The men were dressed in white *kurta* pyjamas with marigold garlands, the ladies in saris, and they looked somewhat bemused. A flurry of fireworks from the roof pfutted and pfopped, then the façade of the palace dramatically came alight with hundreds of tiny bulbs etching the outline of windows, doors, arches and stairs (*see previous pages*). The crowd exhaled as one, the wail of a Rajasthani pipe pierced the night air, and a drummer struck up a traditional welcome song. A tall Rajput, dressed in white with an orange turban, the end of which fluttered down his back like a lick of fire, placed the *tilak* on each guest's forehead and murmured a greeting. The group was ushered onward and upward—to cocktails, entertainment, dancing and dinner.

Such welcomes can't have been that different a hundred years ago at Samode Palace, I reflected. When the *rawal sahib* (the hereditary title of the owner) had to receive an important delegation, he would have waited in his red-and-gold reception room, and the same sort of ritual would have occurred outside. Then the guests would have been ushered into his presence; courtesies would have been exchanged, refreshments offered, *nautch* dances danced, business discussed. The only difference would have been that the ladies wouldn't have accompanied the men; they'd have been secreted up to the *zenana* above the Durbar Hall where frescoed walls, slatted windows and curtains would have concealed their presence from the men. They would have been able to watch proceedings below; but nobody would have caught a glimpse of them.

"Receptions in the past would have been much the same," concurred Lalit Singh Sisodia, the general manager of sister hotel in Jaipur, Samode Haveli. "Except there would have been more people. All the local people would have joined the procession, and there would have been men on horseback, and camels—maybe even elephants." He sat back and sighed theatrically. "Still, we can't have elephants nowadays, and by doing these gala evenings, we are keeping traditions alive." Indeed they are. There's a global fascination with this particular era of Indian history that spans generations. The BBC's adaptation of *The Far Pavilions* was filmed at Samode in the 1980s, and proved immensely popular. Partly because of this appeal and partly because much of the palace had been restored for the cameras, the owners decided to open the palace to tourists. Thus the future of their family seat was secured.

Hari Singh Karigar, a master painter of Rajasthani miniatures, was roped in to help with the restoration work on the palace frescoes. He lives in a richly decorated house in the village, and his

grandson, Chantush, has a shop in Samode's outer courtyard. Chantush explained how his family of painters (six generations of them) worked on the frescoes in the Durbar Hall, the *zenana* and the Sultan Mahal, the private chambers of the family. The latter is particularly noteworthy, with blue-and-silver low-level seating, blue-toned scenes of Indian mythology, flora and fauna, and exquisite mirror work. According to Chantush, only natural paints are used; the family create these themselves by grinding rocks from the surrounding mountains with the gum of certain trees to produce the brilliant peacock blues and greens, and royal reds and golds.

Not only were the frescoes repaired, much work was also done on the basic fabric of the building. After all, it *is* over 450 years old. Built by Rawal Bairi Sal, finance minister to the founder of Jaipur, Raja Jai Singh II, Samode Palace is a classic example of Rajput-Mughal architecture, with its Naples yellow walls and white trim, arches, kiosks and parapets. Both public and private areas are arranged around a series of courtyards on different levels. A relatively recent addition in the forecourt of the Durbar Hall is a swimming pool and Ayurvedic health center and gym. Sensibly enough, the pool is soft-contoured and somewhat old-fashioned in style—a veritable marble-and-mosaic pleasure pool, surrounded by loungers and set in a leafy, walled garden. Slipping into its milky cerulean water after a camel trek in the hills is immensely soothing.

And one thing is certain: the welcome is assured. Whether you get the beefed-up Rajasthani reception, or a simple dignified salute, you'll be the recipient of time-honored Rajput hospitality. At Samode Palace, the glorious past is a constant present.

Samode Haveli, Gangapole, Jaipur 302 002, Rajasthan, India
telefax: +91 141 263 2407/1942/1068/0943   fax: +91 141 263 1397/2370
email: reservations@samode.com   www.samode.com

Rajvilas   Jaipur, India

I notice that the temple doors are open, and glimpse a flash of white inside. The priest has come—as he does each morning and evening of every year. I cross the bridge, remove my shoes and enter the sanctum with head bowed. We exchange greetings, then he points out the Ganesh statue, the central Parvati one, Brahma on the left and his *nandi* in front. At the center is the Shiva *lingum*. I lower my head to receive his blessing, and I offer the shrine some rose petals, then withdraw to the sound of the priest singing: "*Ommm, Shiwaaa, ommm…*" It's curiously calming—he has a tranquilizing voice.

In front of me, the sun is setting and the sky has taken on the tone of light biscuit; at this time of day the pink in the sandstone bridge becomes more pronounced. The water lilies are tucking in their petals; they're going to bed. The priest and I smile shyly at each other and together we look at the sky. The fortress on one side is silhouetted against the evening sky, and a *chattri*, or open Rajasthani pavilion, rises in front of me. Time is suspended—momentarily.

I could be in any temple in Rajasthan, right? Wrong. I'm at the center of Mr PRS Oberoi's dream resort, the much lauded Rajvilas which opened in 1998. The fort houses the reception and public rooms; the *chattri* overlooks the swimming pool and spa. We are standing amongst 32 acres (13 hectares) of landscaped garden, a green oasis within a sandy, dry desert. At the center of it all is the 250-year-old temple, and the priest and I viewing the evening sky.

Any other hotelier may have razed the temple to the ground, but not Mr Oberoi. His respect for the traditions of India are evident not only in his retention of shrine, priest and *puja*, but in all aspects of the lovingly crafted Rajvilas resort. In the same way that Sawai Jai Singh II built Jaipur with its pink sandstone buildings along the lines of a *mandala* or religious diagram with a grid of straight avenues surrounded by a crenelated wall, so did Oberoi's design team at Rajvilas. Here, the main building is a faithful recreation of a Rajasthani fort (*right*), the suites, rooms and villas are laid out like a leafy maharajah's city with the temple at the center, and outside the "walls" is a desert encampment of luxurious tents.

Traditional craftsmanship is seen everywhere. Eight hundred workers labored for three years under Bombay-based architect Prabhat Patki and Malaysia-based interior designer Jeffrey A Wilkes of Lim, Teo + Wilkes Designworks to recreate an estate fit for a maharajah. A lime plaster finish painstakingly applied on the outer walls of the main fort building creates exactly the right soft pink hue, while interior walls are covered in a creamy *araish* finish; craftsmen are reluctant to share the secret *araish* recipe, but it is known that ground stone, marble, egg white and tamarind are some of the ingredients. Extensive use was made of Jaipur's famed blue pottery tiles, both in the main swimming pool and other reflecting pools scattered around the grounds. Similarly, stone masons produced over 200 carved pillars and statues, while skilled painters used gold leaf and deep lapis blue vegetable dyes to produce glimmering floral frescoes in key recesses.

Former US president Bill Clinton stayed at Rajvilas' Royal Villa twice, but mere mortals will be extremely comfortable in one of the 54 deluxe rooms. Set in clusters of six around a courtyard with tropical bird frescoes, blue-tiled walls and fountain, they are a blend of colonial and Rajasthani styles. A four-poster canopy bed and recessed window sofa are piled high with soft cushions, cotton *dhurrie* rugs cover cool floors, while wicker baskets and custom-made cabinets conceal TV and mini-bar. The bathrooms have huge sunken marble tubs with a view of a mini garden, a separate shower stall and a great selection of sensuous lotions and potions.

There is also a tented area at Rajvilas (*left and right*), where guests are given the illusion of camping without skimping on luxury. Traditionally the Rajputs were well known for their frequent expeditions into the desert, forest or mountains, either to wage war or to go hunting, so setting up portable tented villages was a part of their lives. At Rajvilas the tented area is significantly different from the main complex. Landscapes turn from green to grey, lawns are replaced with cacti and pebbles, and adobe-style walls with tribal patterns predominate. The "tents" are perhaps best described as super-deluxe canvas chic: with embroidered inner canopies, luxurious furniture and fittings, teakwood floors, and soft fabrics, they are cool cocoons. "We wanted people to really feel the difference between the harsh environment outside, and the cozy softness within," says Wilkes.

Despite these distractions, it is to the main fort building I return again and again, not so much to gaze on the flaming braziers and floating torches in the central courtyard, marvel at the turrets and ramparts, or flip through the wonderful selection of books in the wood-paneled library as for the act of crossing the moat and entering the massive made-by-hand brass door. For once inside, I know I'll be cosseted, pampered and looked after. As with the Rajputs of old, once they crossed their fortified thresholds, they felt safe from the marauding hordes.

Goner Road, Jaipur, Rajasthan 303 012, India
tel: +91 141 268 0101   fax: +91 141 268 0202
email: reservations@oberoi-rajvilas.com   www.oberoihotels.com

Devi Garh   near Udaipur, India

There are literally hundreds of heritage hotels in Rajasthan, but none even nearly meets the superb standard set by Devi Garh. Encased within an 18th century shell lies a hidden 21st century gem; it is, quite simply, in a league of its own. An all-suite, all-white hotel, it shimmers in a cocoon of chic.

This is not immediately apparent, as the exterior of the fort palace is purposely left somewhat rough and ready (*see left and previous pages*). Painted in ochre tones with grey exposed stone, and topped by a profusion of graceful *jarokhas* (protruding balconies), cupolas, pavilions and pillars, its exterior is imposing—but more medieval than modern. You only get an inkling of what is to come once you start the ascent through its series of massive fortified gates. The reception—decked out in black terrazzo, granite and mother-of-pearl—gives an indication that something may be up. But it is only when you enter your suite that all is revealed.

Here you'll be confronted with a poem in stone. My Aravali Suite was a cool, white marble sanctuary, accented with silverwork, *thekri* (a type of mirror work) marquetry and two huge bowls of pink rose petals. Their scent combined with the air-conditioning was mesmeric. The bed, table, sofa, alcoves, bookshelves, mirrors, even decorative pots, ashtrays and vases were all carved out of locally quarried marble. Bed and chair covers were in white cotton, and cast-in-situ terrazzo floors with marble chips encouraged me to immediately kick off my shoes. The series of rooms was wildly tasteful, zen even. They looked stark and ascetic, but were deeply luxurious.

The hotel has 23 such suites, and all are individually styled. Against a meditative canvas of white are certain choice accents. In one, it may be a series of lotus patterns, in another a splash of color in the form of rust-colored silk cushions and striped tiger statues, in another a cascade of flowers carved into the walls. Museum-quality lighting in each hones in on the particular feature to be highlighted, be it a lapis lazuli table top, a relief of carved marble trees set into a wall or a modern interpretation of a *jaali*. The Devi Garh Suite, themed around Shiva and his *vahana* (vehicle), Nandi the bull, is an ode to indulgence with a private jacuzzi, black marble pool and outdoor pavilion.

With the exception of the garden suites and six luxury tents, all suites are sited off a maze of levels, corridors and courtyards within the main palace. Here there are three courts—the Durbar (royal), the Kamal (lotus) and the Zenana, which in times past would have housed the women's chambers. Each is appropriately designed according to its particular theme, and mediates between the rough-hewn, masculine body of the palace and the sensuous, refined interiors. For example, the Zenana court is planted with *parijat* trees (these have feminine symbolic connotations) and white-flowering shrubs, and its off-center womb-like fountain sucks water inward, rather than throw it out.

Also to be found here are the various public rooms. Some have been left much as they were found: a small corner *sheesh mahal* (mirrored hall) has only fragments of mirror and paintwork left intact, and faded frescoes and remnants of carvings, both stone and wooden, are left elsewhere. Other rooms, however, have been completely restyled. The Durbar Hall (*left*), a conference lounge and the billiards room take their cue from the three metals—gold, silver and copper respectively. Each features custom-made pieces that fuse traditional craftsmanship with contemporary designs.

Delhi-based Rajiv Saini was the interior designer. He freely admits that he had never worked on a project of such scale and magnitude, and it took him a few months to crystallize a design strategy. "My aim while restoring the fort palace was not merely to bring the building back to life but to infuse in it an energy that would carry it through the millennium," he says. "In the process, instead of introducing elements which negate the past, I tried to create a dialogue between a sober aesthetic backed by modern technology and the existing structure."

From where I'm sitting, he succeeded…in tons. The majesty of the original building is easily apparent at every turn, yet all the mod-cons are there. Three elevators were installed; there is a fully equipped gym, invigorating Ayurvedic center, sauna and steam rooms in the maharajah's old stables beneath a modernist green marble swimming pool; and in each suite you have internet access, satellite television and CD player, as well as air-conditioning for summer and heating for winter (yes, those Rajasthani nights can get chilly believe it or not). Add to that, meticulous attention to detail, impeccable service, regard for the vernacular idiom and rigorous standards of interior design. Other palaces-turned-heritage-hotels with their clichéd interiors, indifferent food and erratic plumbing could well take a leaf out of Devi Garh's book.

Devi Garh, Village Delwara, Tehsil Nathdwara, District Rajsamand, Rajasthan, India
tel: +91 2953 289211   mobile: ++ 91 94141 70211   fax: +91 2953 289357
email: devigarh@deviresorts.com   www.deviresorts.com

"The only thing I was sure about," says the hotel's interior designer, Rajiv Saini, "was keeping it simple and making it contemporary while respecting the existing architecture. So I began by innovating with local craft traditions and skills, experimenting with new forms and techniques." Over the ensuing months and years (the fort took eight years to restore), stone masons chipped and cajoled various marbles into works of art. The restrained design palette includes both original fixtures, such as *jaali* screens, ceiling moldings and faded frescoes (*above left*), with custom-carved pieces and modern interpretations of age-old forms (*above right*).

Udaivilas Udaipur, India

Einstein once said "the difference between past, present and future is only an illusion"—and nowhere is this more apparent than at Udaivilas. The latest in the "vilas" chain from Oberoi Group, Udaivilas is totally new, but steeped in history; constructed from modern bricks and mortar, but built in the style of the Mewar princes through and through.

If you fly into Udaipur, you'll be picked up at the airport, taken to a jetty and you will arrive at the hotel, as princes did in the past, by boat. If you come by car, however, it's through the fortress-like gates, round a sweeping crescent of driveway, all the while catching glimpses of a huge onion dome here, an open pavilion there, a massive fortified wall elsewhere. Then it's round the corner to alight aside a grandiose metallic fountain shaped like the sun (the Mewari princes claim to be descended from no lesser figure than the Sun God), and into a cool courtyard where water soothes and an old *neem* tree casts both shade and scent. After that it's a short walk to the reception lobby.

Here you are greeted beneath a gigantic cobalt blue dome (the second largest in Udaipur, I'm told), lined with paintings of 32 of India's flowers and lit by a cut lead crystal chandelier. Sumptuous furnishings, a central indoor fountain and the view over the lake to the City Palace on the opposite shore takes your breath away. You're treated to a welcome tailored for royalty. For that is what Udaivilas does: it treats its guests like kings and queens in a palatial environment built in the style of a modern-day Maharana.

The brief, after all, was to build a palace. Set within a breathtaking 32-acre (13-hectare) site on the shores of Lake Pichola, Udaivilas exudes an aura of greatness in the grand Mewar tradition. As with Rajvilas and Amarvilas, the architect was Nimish Patel and he has—once again—risen to the challenge. The sun motif figures prominently, as does a profusion of domes, arches, cupolas and pavilions. In the same way that the royal guesthouse of the Shiv Niwas palace across the lake is crescent-shaped, at Udaivilas there is a large crescent-shaped colonnaded wing, with a carved amphitheater at its center. Elsewhere, reflecting pools, grandiose courtyards and flowing water

interconnect the different buildings into an assimilation of spaces not unlike those found at a traditional Mewar palace.

The interiors, says interior designer Jeffrey A Wilkes, follow "an eclectic collected approach," and take their inspiration from Indian, Anglo-Indian and art deco influences. "Our mission was to complete and complement the image of greatness Mr Oberoi wanted in the architecture," explains Wilkes, "So we used furniture and fabrics from different periods and styles to give the impression that someone had collected the pieces over time, to imply a sense of history and to reinforce the idea of the residential. We wanted to appear timeless. I don't think that there will come a time when someone will walk into any of the many splendid spaces at Udaivilas and say: 'Time to renovate.' Functions and requirements may change, but the interiors are essentially a canvas upon which history will continue to add layer upon layer."

This sense of timelessness permeates through every aspect of Udaivilas. As does the attention paid to the details. The choice of art, artifacts, furniture and furnishings, is well thought through and appropriate. As ceramics are to China, metalwork is to India. Hindus preferred metal vessels as they thought they didn't carry ritual pollution when passed from one caste to another; the Mughals inherited this preference without realizing its origins. Metallic accents in the hotel include the two huge Sun God fountains, large engraved water urns of beaten metal, beaten *bidri* horses in the rooms as well as crow figurines in the bar, amongst others. Similarly, cushions and covers with embroidery, reverse appliqué, quilting and over-stitching reflect the variety of India's textile traditions. Carpets are invariably hand-crafted and custom made, many using tribal patterns and motifs.

One of my favorite places in the resort is the intimate Candle Room that marks the point of transition from the public spaces to the guest wings. Circular and domed, it is a miniature *sheesh mahal*. In any palace, the king would have had at least one such "glass palace" bedroom, whereby fragments of glass or *thekri* work would have covered every surface; as night fell, candles were lit in these rooms to create a flickering, ethereal boudoir of beauty. At Udaivilas, the Candle Room's dome is entirely covered in a shell motif of mirror pieces, beneath which stands a focal table with a huge collection of candlesticks. These act as the sole source of illumination—and create a calming, quiet and wonderfully romantic space when lit.

Such a space almost beggars belief. Who could have conceived such a cocoon? Decades from now Udaivilas' Candle Room will remain as a testament to Mr Oberoi's vision. This type of style simply doesn't date. It will stand, for future generations, as an illustration of greatness.

Haridasji Ki Magri, Udaipur, Rajasthan 313 001, India
tel: +91 294 243 3300   fax: +91 294 243 3200
email: reservations@oberoi-udaivilas.com

As miniature painters of the Mewar School created scenes of the lives of the maharajas of Udaipur using only a single squirrel hair as a brush, at Udaivilas artist Ghanshyam Mimbark and his team have produced wall murals in the traditional manner. Festive processions, elephants (*above*), camels, warriors, kings and commoners adorn suites and corridors in a profusion of life and color. Gold leaf stenciling (*opposite bottom right*) is another traditional craft revived, and Rajasthan's heritage is further reflected in the choice of ornaments, wall hangings, fabrics and furniture.

Fort Tiracol Heritage Hotel Pernem, India

Uniquely situated atop a promontory of green overlooking the Arabian Sea on one side, and the Arondem river estuary and a pristine swathe of deserted beach lined with casuarinas on the other, Tiracol Fort is part fortification, part religious site, part air, part light. It exists in its own space and time on the northernmost tip of Goa, an area rarely reached by tourists. Accessed by pothole-ridden roads, an erratic ferry crossing and a serpentine road up the hill, it stands alone—built as if to withstand both unwanted invaders and time itself.

I first visited Tiracol 20 years ago. The basic structure remains unchanged as it has for centuries: a massive fortified wall with battlements rises from the rock on which it perches, and behind it, a courtyard containing a tiny chapel and larger-than-life statue of Christ with arms outstretched, reminiscent of the statue of Christ in Almada, Portugal. In those days, Tiracol was a government-run guesthouse, wonderfully atmospheric, yet shabby, run-down and woefully neglected. Today, in the hands of the couple that run Nilaya Hermitage in the hills behind Calangute (*see pages 112–121*), it is once again a living, breathing entity oozing history, character and glamor.

The early 18th century fort was captured by the Portuguese in 1776 from the Bhonsles, a Maratha clan, and from then on demarcated the northernmost boundary of Portuguese domain in India—until 1961 that is, when India retook Goa. It's a super-solid structure, made from laterite blocks. Well protected by battlements interspersed with small rotund watch towers topped by pointed finials, it seems to hang suspended between sea and sky. Running down from the wall is a steep pathway that leads to an oval courtyard almost at sea level, lined with gun holes on either side; this is where canon would have been dragged down to fire at attackers from the sea. Today, in more peaceful times, the courtyard is the place to take an early morning cup of tea and watch the dolphins duck and dive in the mouth of the estuary.

In the restoration project, Hari Ajwani and Claudia Derain chose a colonial Portuguese palette of ochre, white and black, along with metallic accents. It's a totally appropriate color scheme for

the building, as it differentiates the structure from the landscape, yet accentuates its earthy individuality. Eighteenth century iron balustrades, built to keep people out, now offer protection on the upper verandah where long rows of ceramic water jars painted black strike a contrast with cascading bougainvillea and whitewashed walls. It's on this spacious terrace that meals are served beneath large white umbrellas; and off this, up a few steps, is the intimate breakfast room and bar. Front-of-house, under the supervision of long-termer Gregory, is friendly and informal. Food is more than likely to be fresh catch of the day: crab curries, fillets of pomfret or kingfish lightly pan-fried in lime, garlic and turmeric, Goan fish curry, and side-dishes of fluffy white rice and vegetables. Fruit and locally made perfumed vanilla ice cream are the usual desserts.

In addition to a complete paint job, Hari and Claudia converted some of the bedrooms into bathrooms or suite rooms, and modernized the antiquated plumbing and lighting. With only five rooms and two suites in total, the hotel now offers an intimacy that befits its size; yet, because the rooms are airy and high-ceilinged, the overall effect is more spacious. "We wanted to preserve a minimalistic fort look inside," explains Claudia, "So we opted to create our own wrought-iron, marble and black teak wood furniture, very straight-lined and simple." Add to this a few choice artifacts—a metal-and-cut-glass wall hanging, tall ironwork candle holders with church candles, a pair of antique glass bottles—and the end result are interiors that are both contemporary yet in keeping with the monumental structure. Bathrooms, which can be cavernous, have black laterite floors, white-tiled or painted stonework, black cracked tiling or polished concrete in the showers, and stainless-steel and porcelain fittings. They are somewhat monastic, yet very effective.

Dramatic and homely in turns, Tiracol is unique. "Hari and I know and love Tiracol from years back," explains Claudia. "We first went there in the early 1970s. So when we heard in June 2002 that the Government of Goa was putting it out for lease, we didn't hesitate for one second. We knew we had to have it!" Unfortunately the structure had deteriorated more than they had anticipated, but hard work and a lively, imaginative design ethos have resurrected the building. In the hands of people who love it, Tiracol is once again prospering.

Undoubtedly one of Tiracol's strengths is the simple fact that you are staying in a former Portuguese fort on the northernmost tip of Goa in splendid isolation. There's a palpable sense of history all around. The fort's elevated position and the views it affords from the ramparts are quite something else. Sitting on the upstairs verandah (or on one of the top-floor rooms' private balconies), gulping in the clean air and panoramic seascapes, is a sublime experiënce. Nonetheless, you cannot be guaranteed total isolation: because Tiracol is a registered National Heritage Site, day trippers come to view the fort and chapel from time to time. But hey, when you're in Paradise, you can afford to share—can't you?

Tiracol, Pernem, Goa 403 524, India
tel: +91 2366 227631
email: nilaya@sancharnet.in

Siolim House   Bardez, India

Siolim House is more family home than hotel, more *palacio* than house, more labor of love than commercial enterprise. In fact, the 275-year-old Portuguese nobleman's residence was originally bought and restored by the owner Varud Sood for his own family's use—and really only became a hotel by chance.

"Converting Siolim House into a hotel came as an afterthought," says the owner. "After the enormous restoration job, we realized that hosting guests would help us keep it in perfect shape, and give to it the character that comes with welcoming people from all over." So, take guests they do, and if you're fortunate enough to stay there, first-hand insights into Indo-Portuguese architecture and the charm of old Goa are your reward. Culturally, and emotionally, a few days sojourn at the house are hugely enriching.

"I've always been interested in Goan architecture," says Sood, "In fact, as a child we were often in Goa as my father was in the Navy." But it was only when he started going there once again on holidays some ten years ago, that the interest turned into a reality. Sood found Siolim House by serendipity, but didn't let its terrible state of disrepair put him off. The main part of the house hadn't been lived in for six years, and the back part for about 50. Goa's monsoons had well and truly done their work—and extensive restorations were necessary.

Up until a decade or so ago, Siolim House had belonged to a prestigious Goan family. Past owners have included the Governor of Macau, whose porcelain china grilles from the East can still be admired in the house, and administrators in Portuguese Mozambique—hence the house is sometimes known as the Mosmimcar or the Mozambican. A two-storey mansion known as a *casa de sobrado*, it is a typical nobleman's mansion: servants and services would have been on the ground floor, while the upper storey was reserved for the lord of the house. This is illustrated by the large wooden flap-door that can be lowered over the wooden staircase, effectively blocking off the upper living quarters. Here, first-floor rooms have high beamed ceilings, intricate tiled or wooden floors and are extremely spacious rooms. The ground floor, in general, sports smaller rooms and lower ceilings.

The hierarchy of the house is also apparent in the façade of Siolim House (*left*): decorative detail on the upper storey's full-height windows is far superior to that of the waist-high, plainer windows below. Overall, the mansion accurately represents Goa's *cha* style, a type of architecture that is characterized by pure, unfrivolous decoration and classical proportions.

The renovation job was enormous. Part of the roof had fallen in, there was a big damp problem, there were structural problems in the rear part, many of the pillars were crumbling and old tiles were cracked or missing. But Sood was determined not to cut corners, and demanded that the house be restored as close to its original condition as was possible. For example, he insisted on sourcing oyster shell from Panjim for the window panes and using pure crushed shell lime wall plaster for the walls—naturally both were far more costly than their modern counterparts, glass and cement. Similarly, Sood was very generous with his use of space; out of the original 24 rooms came only seven rooms, all with en suite bathrooms, a number of reception rooms and halls (*right and below*) and a lot of open public space. In these rooms, he has placed antique furniture pieces and choice artworks that complement the architecture. "I still haven't found everything I'd like," he admits, "but I'm sure the rest will come as Siolim House re-acquires character by virtue of the people who pass through it, rather than as a result of a quick furnishing job."

The result is homely and palatial—in turns. With only one television in the upstairs "games room," no mini-bar, no air-conditioning, no reception to speak of, and even no menu, Siolim House flies in the face of modern hoteliering standards. Yet it offers an alternative that is as beguiling as it is seductive. In the upstairs bedrooms, sun and light filter through the oyster-shell windows onto the enormous four-poster bed. Above, the ceiling is a pattern of wood and tile, the work of artisans whose craftsmanship has lasted through generations. The bathroom is the size of an office board-room. In fact, many of the bathrooms are huge: some even feature the stepped "pig" toilets of

old where pigs replaced the flush; thankfully today modern plumbing has replaced the pigs! Outside, there's a pillared mosaic-tiled courtyard (*overleaf*) that comes complete with gurgling fountain and a garden bursting with bougainvillea with a pool long enough to do laps in. There's the smell of lunch, and the barking of Wag the dog.

Service is wonderfully warm and personal. Meals are *table d'hote*, and because the kitchen is centrally placed amongst the rooms—and its door is always open—its activities are a constant in the day-to-day running of the house. If you like you can accompany the staff on the daily grocery trip to the wharf and the market; or you can opt for a lazy read in the hammock or take a trip to one of the deserted, white-sand northern beaches across the Chapora River. The choice is yours.

For many centuries, guests to India's Portuguese state were received either at one of the large private residences or small inns, lodges and farmhouses akin to the *pousadas* and *quintas* so plentiful in Portugal. Today, with the welcome addition of Siolim House to Goa's hotel scene, the tradition has once again been revived.

Vaddy (opposite Vaddy Chapel), Siolim, Bardez, Goa 403 517, India
tel: +91 832 227 2138/941 fax: +91 832 227 2323
email: info@siolimhouse.com www.siolimhouse.com

A courtyard with Moorish influences (*above*) is a familiar sight in Portuguese *pousadas*, and the one at Siolim House is the original—albeit repaired—thing. Other originals include floors tiled in geometric patterns, wood ceilings, ironwork and genuine, warm hospitality. In deference to the region's history each enormous suite or room is named after a Portuguese trading port of the 17th century.

Nilaya Hermitage   Arpora Bhati, India

Perched on a hillside in Arpora, with a view over the scrub landscape of Goa and out to the vast Arabian Sea, Nilaya Hermitage is an extraordinary creation. Built around a free-form swimming pool on a number of different levels, it literally seems to grow out of the hillside in which it nestles. Built almost entirely from local laterite exposed stone, with a central golden domed relaxation room, it is an ethno-eclectic mix of styles—Moorish, Mediterranean, Mumbai, with more than a nod to Gaudi and colonial Goa.

If that sounds like a hodge-podge—it isn't. Somehow it all seems to work together to form an organic whole. Combined with the architecture is a strong palette of different shades of blue; these, shot through with ochre, orange and metallic accents, give the property a striking originality.

The creative force behind Nilaya Hermitage is Claudia Derain, a French national who previously worked as a fashion stylist in Paris, before meeting Hari Ajwani, and moving to Goa. "The word, *nilaya*, is derived from Sanskrit and roughly translated means 'abode in the blue heaven'," she explains. "I have always been fond of using blue in hot countries—it is a cooling, soothing, relaxing color, ideal for a small boutique hotel where people come mainly to rest and de-stress." At Nilaya, Claudia explores the color in all its tones. There's blue-and-white striped upholstery on the pool loungers; aquamarine cracked tiles in the bathrooms; pale blue terrazzo floors; royal blue washed walls; a turquoise broken-tile mosaic swimming pool—all complemented with elegant wrought-iron furniture, beaten copper lamps, traditional brass pots and jars, and *objects d'art* fashioned with a variety of metallic sheens.

If blue and gold are the predominant colors inside, the exterior is all rugged rock. Architect Dean D'Cruz designed the building in-situ and even though there was an architectural plan, it evolved from the hill setting and changed often as construction went along. It took two-and-a-half years to complete the hotel with 350 people working on the project full time. Porous brownish-red stone sits well with old roof tiles and blends nicely into the earthy setting. Arches influenced by Moorish culture puncture walls, and windows are often topped by a pointed motif. There's a small al fresco breakfast nook centered around teak columns from a temple in Kerala; here hand-crafted metal chairs accompany blue-tiled tables. An outside bar and pavilion-style "dining room" overlook the pool—and, beyond that, to coconut plantations, the sea and finally the horizon. Up in "blue heaven" all is quiet and cool, with wonderful breezes keeping the temperature a good few degrees lower than down on the coast.

There's also a fair degree of New Age stuff going on. The original plan was to build a house shaped like the yin–yang symbol and even though the buildings have been amended and added on to, the hermitage still bears some resemblance to this shape. The hotel's motif is a star, and this is seen in a variety of forms throughout. In the reception area (*left*) its pattern radiates out from a central pillar on the stone floor, while star-shaped sculptures adorn the relaxation room (*overleaf*), and small twinkling "star-lights" punctuate the rotunda roof.

Unlike the starchy, formal reception desks of larger hotels, the reception room at Nilaya is relaxed and casual—and displays lamps, ornaments and jars with a variety of metallic sheens. As well as being heavy on the metal, it also makes a statement with glass and gold bottles and jars, terrazzo and terracotta tones, and a central gold pillar. Dining is casually al fresco, served in the open-sided pavilion above the pool. Unlike many other hotels in Goa, the food comprises fresh salads and soups, a mix of Italian and French with some local ingredients, but in general more geared toward an international audience. When you can't face another curry and rice, it makes for a welcome change. While eating, check out the bottom of the pool—the star-etched mosaic tile pattern makes for meditative munching.

Originally there were only eight rooms at Nilaya, each named after the eight elements of Indian mythology—Air, Fire, Water, Soul, Moon, Sun, Stars, Earth—but four more have since been added. Each is different, with interiors taking inspiration from the individual themes. Furniture and furnishings are stamped with the signature of Claudia's creativity. A cane couch with scrolled edges sits next to a wrought-iron candlestick, while light streams across a deep blue wall. A net-draped colonial four-poster floats on a platform of light, and linens are white, soft and welcoming. A bathroom employs mirror pieces along with cracked turquoise and aquamarine tiles to create a mélange of refracted light, color and life. Since so many of the pieces are designed and custom made by Claudia and her in-house welder, it made sense to start a shop selling the excess. But Sangolda isn't any ordinary shop: it's an old, converted colonial house/gallery, where each room is a constantly changing showcase of handwoven fabrics, one-off antiques, metallic sculptures and art by various painters. Take a suitcase when you go down, that's my advice.

As befits such an individualistic enterprise, a stay at Nilaya Hermitage is about much more than sleeping in a hotel room. The hotel tends to attract creative, arty types, and over Christmas and New Year the parties are legendary. Claudia and Hari are enormously welcoming, and repeat guests make up a large portion of the clientele. There's an adult-only trendiness to the place that is attractive to 30-somethings with careers, sans enfants. And because you're likely to be mixing with interior design gurus, models and music magazine magnates, it helps to know your Gaudi from your Gauguin, your Charles Correa from your Chick.

But don't be put off: Nilaya really is an inspirational place to chill out (it's not called a hermitage for nothing)—and if all that good taste becomes too much, there's always the Brit-pack beer "n" butties brigade down on the nearby coast. I know where I'd rather be.

Arpora Bhati, Goa 403 518, India
tel: +91 832 276793/94   fax: +91 832 276792
email: nilaya@sancharnet.in   www.nilayahermitage.com

Like a Gauguin painting, Nilaya Hermitage nestles within the intense green of the Goan hillside, sparkling with its bright blue tones and eye-catching gold dome. Inside, mosaic patterns, metals and masonry ensure that there is always something to marvel at. Boldly flying in the face of convention, traditional furniture (*above*) is mixed and matched with custom-made and modern pieces.

Pousada Tauma   Calangute, India

Goa is justly famous for its beaches, but with the opening of the Vasco de Gama Airport to charter flights from Europe, many have become horribly built-up and overcrowded. This is especially true in the hippy havens of old at Calangute, Baga and Anjuna, where beach shacks with loud music, over-zealous hawkers, rave-scene clubs, concrete and traffic are now the norm. It's a sad sight for those (myself included) who remember quiet coconut groves, miles of white sand, wonderful Indo-Portuguese architecture—and only the odd traveler or two for company.

Still, times change, but all is not lost. Sitting pretty (and pretty quiet) amidst the mayhem of Calangute is the haven of Pousada Tauma, a small 12-suite boutique hotel. It is really the last place on earth you'd expect to find a personal, rarefied and top-notch resort, but trust me—it's there. Only a kilometer or so from the beach and set within a walled compound, the only sounds here are the trickle of running water and the breeze rustling through the palms. Discovering it is like stepping from Dante's Inferno into Alice's Wonderland.

Because there are no views to speak of, the layout—both conceptually and architecturally—looks inward. Clusters of buildings, constructed from the local laterite stone usually reserved for the foundations of houses, are scattered around a central amoeba-shaped pool. Because each building is individual and each block of stone is irregularly shaped and fits with its neighbors like a jigsaw puzzle, the effect is pleasingly informal. Loosely linked by a series of arches, pavilions, swathes of plants and hardscapes of local pebbles, there are two main buildings housing the reception and Ayurveda center and gym, a more open-plan, pavilion-style restaurant and the suites. Once encased within the compound walls, you get a taste of how Goa was pre-packaged tourism —slow-paced, serene and sybaritic.

The hotel is the brainchild of owner/manager Neville Proença and was born from his "passion for the industry." As he wryly admits, if he hadn't been passionate about hoteliering, he wouldn't have chosen to spend three-and-a-half years battling with banks and builders to see his project to

fruition, then routinely spend 17-hour days on site. After working for 13 years for the Taj Group, the soft-spoken Proença inherited the land from his father—and decided to go it alone. The word *tauma* is a shortened version of his father's name and also loosely translates as "restful"—and this is the experience Proença is keen to offer his guests.

"Nothing is too much trouble," he says, "I have a multi-skilled staff, and our job is to cater to every need of our guests. We offer an extremely personalized service." It is this human touch that sets Pousada Tauma apart from some of its competition.

An advocate of the "small is beautiful" ethos, Proença is constantly looking at ways to improve his product. Swathes of lawn, which required constant watering and encouraged mosquitoes to breed, were recently replaced with river pebbles. After they've been sprayed with water, their dappled surfaces not only look beautiful, they help cool the air. Ceramic roof tiles, sourced from derelict Indo-Portuguese houses, are replaced regularly; not only does their U-shape encourage ventilation, they look a lot prettier than the new ones. The furniture in both the restaurant and the rooms is in large part custom made in copper and metal, and when it was seen that the furniture scratched the Rajasthani floor tiles, small rubberized "feet" were specially made for the legs. Such attention to detail—even if it is time-consuming and non-essential—is characteristic of Proença's labor-of-love attitude.

This individualistic approach is extended to the suites themselves. These are haphazardly arranged around the swimming pool, and each is decorated around a theme of field, sea, hill or castle. The suites come in different shapes, sizes and décor, but each has a bedroom, bathroom, sitting room and a small outdoor terrace with a garden view. Field suites convey the cool feel of bamboo, grass and palm, both in the design on the grilles and windows and in the paintwork stenciling which is echoed in the bathroom tiles. Similarly, the Sea suites evoke the ocean, with octopus, starfish and shell motifs, and cool shades of aquamarine and indigo. Furniture is carefully sourced or custom made to suit—bamboo and cane for the Field rooms, for example, and Goan antiques for the more formal décor of the grander Castle rooms.

Bollywood stars, French nobility, publishing magnates and many others have all experienced the red carpet treatment at Pousada Tauma, and much of Proença's trade now comes from repeat visits and personal recommendations. After all, it's not every hotel that can arrange a personal dog-sitter for a prize pet on New Year's Eve, or a private house-party for a 50th birthday celebration at the drop of a hat.

Porba Vaddo, Calangute, Bardez, Goa, India
tel: +91 832 227 9061/62/63   fax: +91 832 227 9064
email: neville@pousada-tauma.com   www.pousada-tauma.com

Park Hyatt Goa Resort and Spa Cansaulim, India

Situated along one of south Goa's most beautiful beaches, the Park Hyatt is a sprawling low-rise development set over 45 acres (18 hectares) of land fronting the Arabian Sea. Built to echo the elements of a Goan village, the resort architecture borrows elements of Portuguese baroque, complete with columns, vaulted ceilings and even a small chapel. Taking the tones of traditional mansions—a dusky pink that changes from terracotta to rose depending on the time of day, mint green, sky blue and lemon yellow—the resort is a maze of buildings interconnected by bridges, walkways and paths. Set in a landscape that respects the original sand dunes, planted with canna lilies, hibiscus and other tropical ornamentals, it boasts the largest swimming pool in India. It's a serpentine swathe of cool blue that hugs the architecture like the contours of a hill on a map.

Everything you could possibly need on holiday is at hand; set along a ceramic-tiled path functioning as the "main street" is a rotund Portuguese tapas bar, complete with viewing deck equipped with binoculars and telescopes for ocean and star gazing, a library, a Western grill, a *tandoori* restaurant, a wood-fired pizza-and-pasta restaurant, an open-plan bakery, juice bar and *dhosa* bar too. The Camp Hyatt kids' club is packed with programs; there are shops, a photo-developing store, a florist and even a small cinema. The spa with Ayurvedic and other treatments is a cool oasis of Goan mosaics and fountains, and below it, there's a gymnasium and yoga room. There's even a beachside casuarina forest, and dotted within it are platforms designed for quiet meditation.

The resort's main axis runs from the gate entrance straight through the enormous and airy open-sided lobby across pools, a section of the swimming pool and over dunes and coconut grove to Arossim Beach and the sea. On either side are the residential blocks or *pousadas* and the resort plaza, constructed to represent an Indo-Portuguese street. Accommodation includes 13 suites, one of which is a Presidential suite, and a variety of guest rooms, all equipped with high-speed internet access in the rooms and on the spacious verandahs. "If you have to be connected," says the general manager, "why not do so on your own private verandah whilst taking tea?"

Indeed, and it is in large part because of such details that the Hyatt decided to elevate the resort to Park Hyatt status. The top-of-the-range brand in the Hyatt stable, the Parks are noteworthy because of their stylish design, exclusivity and highly personalized service. At the Goa hotel, each guest is allocated a resort guide on arrival: he or she is directly responsible for the stay of that guest, so if there are any problems they can be ironed out quickly.

Conceptual designer Simeon Halstead has tried wherever possible to go local in the overall concept of the resort. The main bar is named after Goan cartoonist Mario Miranda—not only did the artist supply the cartoons on the walls, he takes an active interest in the resort as a whole. This is the place to try Goa's famous tipple, cashew fenny; skillful bartenders have devised a menu of punches and cocktails with this local hooch. Furniture here is made from wood with interwoven straw and hessian cushions; the designer comes from Milan, but the chairs are custom made in India. Similarly, Goan artist Shireen Mody provided the superb painting of light falling on palm fronds in the lobby and smaller versions on the same theme in the bedrooms. Also in the lobby are larger frescoes painted by a local artist, while in the rooms young photographer Fram Petit has provided seascapes and landscapes in black and white.

Many members of staff are locally hired and are friendly and helpful, to the extent that one of our party's toddler was endlessly amused and cosseted while the parents took time out by the pool. Activities for children are fun-filled and varied, and the Serano Spa offers both Indian and Western, modern and traditional therapies in nine indoor treatment rooms and several outdoor mosaic-tiled areas. An assortment of yoga, meditation and spiritual workshops are also offered.

Although accommodation blocks are quite dense, each room is private and self-contained. All feature unusually spacious open-plan revitalization areas that combine the qualities of a standard bathroom with those of a personal spa. There's an enormous, sunken bath with invigorating overhead rain shower; a bit like a Turkish bath, it is tiled in sweet, petite ochre ceramic tiles. Many of the bathrooms overlook miniature secret gardens planted with brilliant flowering shrubs and local fruit trees. Some bathrooms even feature their own outdoor showers.

Even though there are 251 rooms and suites in total at the Park Hyatt, the complex doesn't seem crowded. This is certainly a tribute to the designer and to the personalized service of the staff; they help you, as an individual, to feel special—a rare quality in such a large resort.

Arossim Beach, Cansaulim, South Goa 403 712, India
tel: +91 832 272 1234   fax: +91 832 272 1235
email: parkhyattgoa@hyattintl.com   www.hyatt.com

Rooms and suites (*left*) are spacious and soothing. Sandalwood-scented toiletries are presented
in locally made deep blue ceramic containers. Made by Indian firm Forest Essentials, the exotic
perfumed soap comes with a banana leaf wrapping that encourages you to take it home with you.
Also individual to the resort are the shallow copper dishes overflowing with lush, golden marigolds—
a signature sight.

The Verandah in the Forest Maharashtra, India

"Do you believe in God?" asked my horseman, as he guided me through leafy bridle paths en route to the hotel. We had covered the gamut of conversational pleasantries that are *de rigueur* in India—home, family, profession—and were now approaching the metaphysical. Why not, I felt? It seemed a perfectly sensible question in the circumstances.

Looking around me, it would be difficult not to believe in God. I had left the dusty plains around Bombay some two hours previously, survived precipitous hairpin bends to ascend some 700 meters (2,300 feet) to the last British hill station of Matheran, and was now ambling through an old *jamun* forest on horseback. The air was cool, the atmosphere tranquil, the conversation pleasant. Shards of sunlight filtered through the canopy onto the red earth in front of us. Umesh came from five generations of horsemen, and was clearly more at home in the saddle than on *terra firma*; his two-year-old boy was already riding, and he himself could ride side-saddle, upside down, standing up, how ever. "I am a professional rider," he declared.

And indeed he was. Also, as a local, he was the perfect person to tell me about Matheran. Meaning "jungle-topped," Matheran is one of a swathe of hill stations that are found at elevation all over the Indian subcontinent. During the days of the Raj, such places were developed by British civil servants as holiday retreats. When the heat and humidity became too intense on the plains, first the *memsahibs* and children, and later the menfolk, flocked to the hills. In 1850, Matheran was "discovered" by the then Collector of the region, Hugh Mallet, and inaugurated as a hill station by Lord Elphinstone, the Governor of Bombay, a year later.

Most hill stations are indelibly impressed with their British heritage, and Matheran is no exception. Nineteenth century bungalows set within private grounds with names like Shaw House, signs to One Tree Hill and lookout points called Louisa Point and Porcupine Point, a lake named after a lady called Charlotte speak volumes about the past; there's a narrow gauge railway to reach the hill station, a sweet church and railway station, all relics of an earlier era.

The hotel we were heading for is called the Verandah in the Forest. It's a relatively new addition to the Neemrana Group's stable of "non-hotel hotels." Originally known as the Barr House after the British family that built it in the 1850s, the property certainly lends itself to large house parties, or smaller groups of individuals. It has an informal clubbiness to it; it's like staying in someone's (albeit rather grand) vacation villa where meals are leisurely, you can wander out for a walk or simply put your feet up and snooze or read on one of the most expansive verandahs I've ever seen.

It is known that the house used to be in the hands of the British for some time, but was sold to a wealthy Parsi family in 1927. This family used the house quite a bit for the first 20 years or so, but after that it became practically redundant—in the hands of an elderly caretaker, it was locked to the outside world. A friend of the family advised Neemrana when the owners wanted to sell the property, and partners Francis Wacziarg and Aman Nath visited the site in 2001. "When I first saw [the] Barr House, I just loved it," says Wacziarg. "It wasn't in very good shape, there were no bathrooms, the furniture was very dilapidated—but I knew it was special."

The house itself is a wood-and-brick affair, built to classical proportions. There's a jut-out porch complete with original stained-glass decoration with steps leading up to the verandah, which runs the entire length of the house. Balustraded in wrought-iron that has unfortunately been painted pale lemon (as has the house, albeit rather more successfully), it is appropriately furnished with cane loungers and planters' chairs. Rooms are situated off this verandah, as they are on the floor below. The main reception room is accessible from the porch: yellow-and-white striped wallpaper, an arched double-height ceiling, dark wood furniture, pictures from the days of the Raj, as well as comfortable seating nooks, are all illuminated by stained-glass windows in the ceiling above. A saloon-style door of glass sporting faded birds and flower paintings leads you into the handsome dining room. Dominated by an immense teak dining table with silver candelabra, this is the only formal room in the house.

"We are very minimalistic in our restorations," says Wacziarg. "We try to keep things as much as possible as they were." In addition to putting in new bathrooms, solar panels for water heating and a staff quarters, the new owners had a team of 17 carpenters on site for four months, restoring and polishing the existing furniture, and completing minor repairs. The result is entirely in keeping with the spirit of the house: you sleep soundly in four-poster beds, lounge on re-upholstered chaise loungers, write letters at wonderful old armoires and read beneath original light fittings. Fans whirr lazily overhead and ceramic tiles—faded now, but still showing their beautiful geometric patterns—are cool and comfortable underfoot.

Barr House, Matheran 410 102, District Raigarh, Maharashtra, India
tel: +91 2148 30296
email: sales@neemranahotels.com   www.neemranahotels.com

The Park Hotel Bangalore, India

It is fitting that India's Silicon City is home to one of the Park Group's newer properties. In the same way that Bangalore is forward-looking and high-tech, the Park is high-style and 21st century. Yet as Bangalore continues to honor its past—with well-tended parks, a Botanical Gardens and British-built government and high court buildings—so too does the Park Hotel. Within its contemporary, cosmopolitan interior lies a celebration of Karnataka's history, craftsmanship and culture.

As soon as you arrive, you know that you're in for something different. The pristine white, linear exterior has computer-script signage, boxy stands of bamboo and, if it is night, diffused lighting—all of which display a singular modernity (*top left*). Large glass doors allow for a seamless entrance into the lobby, a compact area entirely sheathed in floor-to-ceiling curtains of aquamarine raw silk, a fabric that Bangalore is famous for. A few choice pieces of leather furniture from Pierre Paulin and Thonet complement the textural space. The *pièce-de-résistence*, however, is a ceiling-high rosewood central pillar, which is a copy of the stone pillars at the ancient capital of the Hoysala dynasty at nearby Hampi; it was carved by descendants of such masons, but this time in wood. Eye-catching in the extreme, it symbolizes the Park Group's commitment to innovative and quality hotel design.

The hotel interiors were designed by the UK's Conran & Partners, with the aim of fusing the vibrant colors, landscapes and culture of India with an international style. At first glance, you think you could as likely be in the US as in India, but closer inspection reveals a strong sense of place. General Manager Lemuel Herbert explains, "Moving away from the idea of the opulent luxury hotel to this modern offering has been a mindset challenge for people in India. Getting the local people to appreciate something that looks apparently so Spartan, but has a lot of understated luxury, has been interesting to say the least."

Certainly, the hotel challenges on many levels. Ambient sounds not so much play as pervade throughout the hotel on a state-of-the-art sound system. Staff members wear uniforms designed by a well-known Bangalore designer; floral arrangements are by a hip, young florist. Service is more casual (yet friendly and efficient) than is often the case in many of India's five-star hotels, where the culture can be somewhat intimidating. "There's a personalized touch in everything we do," says Herbert. "Our staff are multi-skilled and we find this encourages innovation."

A strong urban feeling is created throughout by superior lighting techniques and geometric lines, be it on the logo (a collage of threads), striped carpets, or strong angles in the architecture. Similarly long and thin is the lap pool, the only temperature-controlled pool in Bangalore, and the streamlined gazebos lining the pool are cubes of cool. Here, boxy loungers made from woven cane and upholstered in cream complete with bright scatter cushions and bolsters (*right*), make for a cool al fresco relaxing spot in the early morning or evening. Below the pool, the small gym and treatment rooms, sauna and steam room, decked out with aqua-tiles, entice with an atmosphere of calm and quiet.

The disregard for formality is another of the hotel's characteristics. For example, executive chef Abhijit Saha—who was voted one of India's top ten chefs in 2002 by popular magazine *Outlook*—aims to break barriers in the way food is served. His forte is creative, innovative cuisine with a focus on simple presentation and subtle flavors. The highlight of the 24-hour restaurant, Monsoon, is the long "sharing table" (*right*) that juts into the lobby at an angle; single guests are encouraged to use this table. The dominant color theme here is sunset orange and midnight blue, suggestive of India's rainy season. Orange ceiling lights are echoed by similarly colored glasses on the tables, and both blue and orange upholstery on the chairs. Smaller tables with high-backed woven cane chairs, white crockery and sleek cutlery surround the large angled sharing table.

The hotel bar, aptly named the i-bar, is a multi-sensory experience in itself. Lounge lizards will find themselves right at home with the low-level seating and—for the truly slack—bean-bags whose round shapes are echoed by bulbous floor lights. In true deconstructionist decorative style, one wall is covered with a multi-colored carpet embedded with TV screens, showing anything

from movies to cricket to ads. Hot neon lights above the bar itself, and softer lighting elsewhere, contribute to the techno-electric feel. Cat Stevens at a useful volume, or the latest sounds, and a DJ six nights a week, contribute to the high-energy atmosphere.

The only downside to this hotel is that the rooms are a tad on the small side. Nonetheless, many have balconies, and they are sleek and comfortable. Each room has internet and fax ports, a dark wood working desk with anglepoise lamp, modern four-posters with custom-made 10-inch spring mattresses and goosedown feather pillows, along with signature silk curtains and bed-spreads. Each of the four floors follows a natural decorative theme along with a duo of colors that is repeated in the fabrics, carpets and paintwork on the balconies. A thoughtful addition in each bathroom is a hidden night-light below the sink that provides soft tonal lighting—a serene touch.

The Park Hotel, Bangalore, is ultimately a city hotel. It bills itself as a boutique hotel in the sense that it is a rather smaller, compact hotel with a very distinct identity. In much the same way that a boutique is specialized and design-worthy, so is this hotel. In that aspect it is ahead of its time, especially in India, and will no doubt spawn copies. But right now it is unique in Bangalore —and deserves to be patronized as such.

14/7 Mahatma Gandhi Road, Bangalore 560 042, India
tel: +91 80 559 4666   fax: +91 80 559 4029
email: tpbl@theparkhotels.com   www.theparkhotels.com

Shalimar Spice Garden Resort Murikaddy, India

Ayurveda is an intricate system of healing that originated in India thousands of years ago. Derived from two Sanskrit words, *ayu* which means "life" and *veda* which means "the knowledge of," it is a wholistic practice that aims to provide guidance regarding food and lifestyle so that healthy people stay healthy and not-so-well people improve their health. By health, practitioners don't simply refer to physical wellness: they mean emotional, spiritual and mental equilibrium too.

Ayurvedic doctors believe that the environment in which we live plays a key part in our health. Noisy, crowded and frenetic places tend to produce frazzled nerves and stressed-out people. Conversely, seclusion, quietude and clean air are calming, de-stressing and soothing. This is where the Shalimar Spice Garden Resort comes in. Situated 9 kilometers (5 miles) from the Periyar Tiger Reserve and Wildlife Sanctuary, at the end of a rough-and-ready track, it's a tranquil idyll in the gently undulating hillscapes of Kerala's Western Ghats. Here, in a wild 6-acre (2.4 hectare) spice and fruit-tree plantation, you can foster your *doshas*, indulge in a bit of *rasayana* (anti-ageing therapy) and massage—and generally nurture tired bodies and over-active minds.

Variously described as a "sanctuary for the senses," a "testament to love" and "a holiday hideaway," the resort (although the word is rather misleading here) is the brainchild of Italian architect Maria Angela Fernhof and her Indian yoga instructor partner Shaji. Even though Fernhof has now sold out, Shalimar began as a combination of their names—and their skills. When they first came to the site in 1996, the couple discovered an area of dense Indian forest grown wild. But because it was high in the Cardamom Hills some 760 meters (2,500 feet) above sea level, the air was cool, butterflies and songbirds punctuated the sky and they could see its potential.

Months of hard work followed, but the end result was worth the effort. Seven cottages, built in the local Malayalam style cling to the hillsides at different elevations, offering 15 rooms. Some have teak or rosewood door frames taken from old houses, others mimic the decorative carved pieces of old. Each is different, but all are united in their use of natural materials—wood, thatch, local stone—and contemporary styling. Every room has an en suite bathroom with copious amounts of hot water (wonderful after a strenuous yoga session), but they vary in configuration. Some of the suites have a living room and balcony as well as a bedroom, while other simpler rooms have a monastic platform bed, an old almirah and perhaps an area for lounging. Floors and walls are whitewashed, giving the interiors a clean, modernist look, but local fabrics, stained glass and Keralan knick-knacks inject more than a whiff of the vernacular.

This strong sense of place is most evident in the public spaces. The reception area, dining room and open loggia are all built in the traditional Keralan pattern around a rectangular inner courtyard. Accessible by a swinging wooden suspension bridge straddling a lily pond, they are open structures with wooden or bamboo pillars and thatched roofs. Traditional South Indian accessories complement the architecture: the large wooden rice storage boxes or *orpahayam*, wooden *masala* bowls, salt vessels or *kalpetty* and the long, narrow wooden vessels known as

thonimaravis dot the landscape. The restaurant is a particular delight: tables and benches are shaped out of carved rocks and you are as likely to have a South Indian curry served on a banana leaf as a bowl of fresh pasta with basil and Italian olive oil. Either way, it is heart-warming, fulfilling fare. Fruit and veggies are more often than not locally grown, and home-grown organic coffee beans make a mean cup of coffee.

It is not only the cuisine that is nurturing here. So, too, is the Ayurvedic Centre. That, combined with the general well-being that comes as a result of being in a beautiful, quiet spot, is the main reason for coming here in the first place. Built along the proscribed principles laid down in the Veda, using handmade brick walls, an open fire and stone floors, the center offers a variety of healing and restorative treatments. Because there are a number of fully qualified Keralan specialists here, you'll feel secure in both their diagnoses and their recommendations for treatment. If you have the time and inclination, the purgative Pancha Karma therapy is well-managed, but for those on a tighter time schedule and simply in need of some R & R, the invigorating synchronized massage given by two therapists in tandem is high on my A-list of massage experiences. Expect the exotic, and end up euphoric. Afterward, your renewed energy, combined with the fresh mountain air, makes you feel you can tackle just about anything.

Being at the center of the Spice Hills has its advantages. After all, it was the plentiful output of black pepper, cardamom, cinnamon and other spices that enticed Portuguese and Arab traders to Kerala centuries ago—and the export continues. Nevertheless, the spices are also vital within local communities, and comprise ingredients for herbal medicines, Ayurvedic therapies and Keralan cuisine. At the Shalimar Spice Garden Resort, chefs and doctors alike literally pluck bounty from the trees and shrubs around them. Beat that if you can.

Murikkady P O, Kumily-685 535, Idukki District, Kerala, India
tel: +91 4869 222132/3232   fax: +91 4869 223022
email: shalimar_resort@vsnl.com, shalimarresort@eth.net
www.shalimarkerala.com

The Malabar House Fort Cochin, India

Joerg Drechsel, the brains behind the beauty of bijou boutique hotel the Malabar House, comes from a design exhibition background—and it shows in every detail of his hotel. In the same way that Kerala has a multi-cultural society, taking influences from the Chinese and Arab traders and the Portuguese, Dutch and later British settlers as well as its indigenous populations, the Malabar House showcases elements from past and present, East and West. Sited in a colonial mansion fronting Fort Cochin's old parade ground (where you can watch cricket, football or other sports from the upstairs verandah), it is an intriguing mix of the old and the new.

"In the same way that at an exhibition you have clients for two hours, here in the hotel, we have guests for 24 or more," explains Drechsel. "We want to offer them a multi-layered experience." This is evident from the minute you leave the hot, dusty street outside, and step into the cool front garden of the Malabar House. Walk through the shaded *porte-cochère*—thoughtfully decked out with cane table and chairs—and into an airy, spacious reception hall that has been painted in fashionable ochre tones.

The first thing you see is a statement-making, modern spiral staircase leading up to the first floor. The rough-textured steps are an imaginative decorative device, but they were borne out of necessity. All the concrete for the central spine was mixed manually and stone masons from Tamil Nadu shaped each tread by hand. Once your eyes adjust, you notice the plunge pool and airy, restful internal courtyard (*left*) behind. Hot tones, and cool blue beyond.

All the public areas in the Malabar House radiate from this central axis. Drechsel describes it as "communication architecture," because it is in these spaces that guests have a chance to meet one another. There is the Malabar Junction restaurant on one side, and a newer block of rooms on the other, and within the courtyard itself, loungers and chairs are strategically positioned round the inviting pool. "Many of our guests have met each other here, and remained friends," says Drechsel. "Then they come for a repeat visit."

It is this combination of intimacy and space that is so appealing. The elegant proportions of the Malabar House architecture are juxtaposed with a fresh palette of distressed paint finishes in ochre, blue and hot pink on certain choice walls. Signature art pieces, sourced both locally and abroad, are placed at strategic points. Kerala has a huge tradition of crafts, and Drechsel believes that a well-designed craft solution is often more successful than an industrially designed one. Masks, prows of boats from Fort Cochin's boatyards, statues from the panoply of Hindu gods and goddesses, even a wooden horse used in temple processions, are all thoughtfully displayed. Nothing looks out of place. Even though there is a striking modernity to much of the interior décor, all is set firmly in the vocabulary of the local.

This highly tailored approach is continued in the 17 rooms. These are extremely comfortable and have both individually controlled central air-conditioning and natural ventilation in the form of private open-air terraces or verandahs, providing the instant allure of inside–outside tropical living.

Furniture is a mix of contemporary crafted and antique colonial pieces. Beds may have legs from an old Brahmin cot, with a few extra feet both on the length and width, added by a carpenter to accommodate bigger frames. State-of-the-art lighting with dimmer switches, eclectic art pieces and locally woven textiles complete the scene.

Malabar Junction, the hotel's open-sided restaurant, is located so as to catch the sea breezes in the evenings. Under the direction of Txuku Drechsel, the emphasis is on fresh, locally sourced ingredients—fish, prawns and vegetables—cooked using some of the famous flavors of Kerala's spice trade but with classical European techniques. Pasta is home-made every day, and the only imported item is olive oil. The kitchen often hosts guest chefs from around the globe—and the experience is described as mutually beneficial to both the hotel chefs and the outsiders. Madhur Jaffrey spent a couple of months in the kitchen while shooting a movie in Kerala.

As befits an intimate boutique hotel, members of staff at the Malabar House are extremely helpful, courteous and knowledgeable. It is their belief that they are the link between the local situation and you, the guest, so don't be surprised if you're invited on an outing by the manager, Mr Francis, or you're given a walking tour of the surrounding area. It's all part of the special personalized service.

At night, the hotel takes on a totally different, dramatic veneer. As dusk falls, suffused night-time lighting transforms the public areas and sea breezes filter through the courtyard. Kathakali dance performances or Indian music recitals may be enjoyed on the small stage set between stone pillars resurrected from a nearby temple. The bright pink tones of the restaurant walls stand in brilliant contrast to the underwater lighting of the pool. An evening stroll around the parade grounds and over to St Francis Church is an experience not to be missed. As you return, you'll catch sight of the illuminated mansion from across the green, and for an illusory moment it will seem almost as if the façade were glowing.

1/268–9 Parade Road, Fort Cochin 682 001, Kerala, India
tel: +91 484 221 6666   fax: +91 484 221 7777
email: info@malabarhouse.com   www.malabarhouse.com

The Brunton Boatyard Fort Cochin, India

Built on the site of the former boat-building yard of George Brunton & Sons, this handsome hotel was designed in the style and principle of Fort Cochin's early 16th–17th century Portuguese and Dutch architecture. With a stunning setting along the harbor overlooking the busy ship channel and Willingdon Island, the Brunton Boatyard is a fitting tribute to the spice traders of the Malabar Coast—and the boat builders who outfitted them.

All 22 rooms and four suites overlook the water. You can take the hotel's resident boat that was built in the original boatyard and has now returned home, for a trip round the harbor. Admire the Chinese cantilevered fishing nets, aptly described as "mechanical herons" and introduced together with the wok and the conical hat through early trade with China. Or simply sun yourself on the poolside terrace (*bottom left*), cooled by breezes from the Arabian Sea, and dream of Arab dhows, Spanish galleons and the maritime trade of yore. The sailors of the past swore that a blind man could steer a vessel right into dock at Fort Cochin harbor when the wind blew offshore.

A nautical feeling aptly permeates the entire hotel. Rooms and suites are shipshape chic, with colonial-style and antique furniture in Portuguese mango wood and textiles in white and navy blue. Spacious and uncluttered, no two look alike. Many of the fittings, such as the ceiling fans and doorbells are originals, sourced from old houses in Fort Cochin and Matancharry. Every room has a balcony with sea view, four-poster bed with a little stool for climbing, a lounging area, and some have squares of colored glass in the windows. Suites follow the same theme, but are much larger. White-tiled, modern bathrooms are spacious enough to house both a shower and a bath.

Behind the outward simplicity, however, lies a wealth of substance. Months of research into both architectural styles and building techniques have resulted in a truly outstanding three-storey building. Rectangular in shape, it is set around a central grassy courtyard with a sprawling rain-tree —as was the original boatyard. Surrounding the courtyard are cloister-like corridors, punctuated with picture windows with inset love-seats on one side and small-shuttered windows sourced from Fort Cochin's Jewish area on the other. Walls are painted with Madras *chunam* plaster—a material much used by the British in their former colonies—and described by the 19th century colonial engineer Major JFA McNair as "made from shell lime without sand; but with this lime we had white of eggs and coarse sugar or 'jaggery,' beaten together to form a paste and mixed with water in which the husks of coconuts had been steeped..." Similarly, floors are of red oxide, again used extensively by colonial architects. Dotted around are huge Chinese earthen storage jars.

The front of the building is at once imposing and welcoming. A semi-circular driveway sweeps up to the entrance *porte-cochère* (*left middle*), behind which is the hotel lobby. Built to resemble the interior of the nearby St Francis Church, the oldest church in Fort Cochin and resting place of Vasco da Gama, it has working *punkah* fans and exposed wooden ceiling beams in Indonesian teak. Whitewashed walls are lined with portraits of eminent historical figures from the Dutch, Portuguese and British eras, and there are also some black-and-white photos of the old boatyard.

Kerala has taken influences from many different nationalities over the centuries and this is reflected in its architecture, culture, language—and cuisine. At the Brunton Boatyard the tastes and flavors of many typically Keralan delicacies are celebrated in style. You can try the delicious *rasam* of the Tamil Brahmins, an excellent appetizer, and *sabudana vada*, a Kutchi sago cutlet. There are Konkani dishes such as the *patravada*—made of colaccasia leaves spread with rice paste and steamed in a roll—of which there exist many variations: Memon, Christian, Jewish and Malabari. Muslim fish, chicken and meat specialities, Gujarat's legendary mixed vegetable dish *undhyo* and the roasted chickpea with lamb Mulligatawny soup are all delicious. All these (and more) are available at either the restaurant History, or the adjacent Terrace Grill, where seafood barbecues are also served at wrought-iron, white painted tables and chairs (*see previous page*).

Because there are no extant buildings in Kerala more than 500 years old, it is impossible to determine exactly how the early Dutch and Portuguese structures would have looked. But with the help of archival sources and a plethora of both original and copied fixtures and fittings, the Brunton Boatyard must be about as authentic in style, atmosphere and architecture as is possible. The attention to detail is staggering—and contributes in large part to the successful design of the entire complex.

Fort Cochin, Kerala 682 001, India
tel: +91 484 221 5461-65   fax: +91 484 221 5562
email: brunton@vsnl.net   www.casinogroup.com

Coconut Lagoon Kumarakom, India

"Someone once said that the secret to success in the hotel industry was a room with a view," says Jose Dominic, CEO of the family-owned and family-run Casino Group, one of Kerala's major hotel players. "But we look at it a bit differently and say, how does the room look from the view?"

Cryptic perhaps, but commonsensical and conservation-savvy too. He continues: "Of course you need the aesthetics, the pretty picture, the good food, and so on. But increasingly you need to merge that with the natural environment, and the environment must be used sustainably with the local community."

Not exactly ground-breaking news to NGOs in the eco-know, but unusual (and encouraging) for a big hotel group. And true to its word, Coconut Lagoon delivers. Set in a coconut grove at the point where the Kavanar River meets the eastern shore of Lake Vembanad, it's found deep in the heart of Kerala's green and gracious backwater country. It's a riverine resort, accessible only by boat; there's a complete network of working irrigation channels as well as a free-form swimming pool interspersed amongst the palms, fruit trees and flowering allamanda shrubs—and you lose count of how many times you cross a little bridge. Land and water are inseparable here.

The natural setting is pristine. Rooms are in authentic Keralan cottages, and the public areas, such as the restaurant and jetty/reception, shop and games room, are housed in larger local structures—all rescued from demolition in the early 1990s. The hotel group employed members of the old house-building guild to source Brahmin or *tharawad* houses earmarked for destruction, dismantle them, number all the pieces, transport them by boat to the site, and re-erect them. Some were modified to suit their new requirements, while others were simply rebuilt. Though the cottages vary in configuration, each has a large wraparound verandah, open-air bathroom and cool, airy interiors. All are wood structures made from the local hardwood *anjali* tree; secured on stucco brick platforms, they come complete with original carvings. Worn smooth over the centuries (some of the buildings date from the 1700s), the wood has developed an attractive patina over time.

Interestingly they represent a school of architecture that came to influence vernacular forms as far afield as Southeast and East Asia. Nonetheless, the resort is much more than a showcase of Kerala's built heritage. As an eco-friendly resort, its most significant investment is in a state-of-the-art water purification and sewage treatment system, and solar panels are used to heat water. One of its aims is to preserve and display the local biodiversity: the hotel is experimenting with a field of organically grown rice and many of the planted fruit trees are named, with both botanical and common names. Guinea fowl and ducks peck and preen themselves amongst flowering shrubs, while local Vechoor cows, renowned for their milk (not very high yielding but full of goodness) replace the need for a lawn mower. There's a first-class Ayurveda center, and a butterfly garden.

Whether you're aware of the environmental ethos or not, there is no denying that Coconut Lagoon is a special place. It offers unparalleled access to the backwaters, and seems to exude a spirit all of its own. *National Geographic Traveller* magazine once described Coconut Lagoon as representing "the kind of architecturally and aesthetically sound tourism now rare elsewhere in India," and this has more than a ring of truth to it. More recently, celeb guests Heather Mills and Paul McCartney wrote after their stay: "The staff were warm, kind and very, very welcoming...the food was exceptional...the view under the stars was breathtaking." I echo the sentiments.

Coconut Lagoon, Kumarakom, Kerala, India
tel: +91 481 252 4491
email: casino@vsnl.com   www.casinogroup.com

Hotel de l'Orient Pondicherry, India

Pondicherry, known locally by the affectionate abbreviation "Pondy," is a small coastal town some three hours' drive south of Chennai (Madras). It was the capital of the French colonies in India from the 17th century onward and its attractive colonial quarter still retains a Gallic atmosphere: on a grid of straight, clean streets there are old road signs in French, dilapidated French institutions and monuments in tones of cream and yellow, pink and grey, imposing Catholic churches and a mini Arc de Triomph, built during the time of Napoleon III. Statues of Joan of Arc and French governors are set in squares bursting with flamboyant bougainvillea. This is also the area that houses the sprawling premises of the famous Sri Aurobindo Ashram. The town is slightly off the beaten tourist track—and many argue that this simply serves to accentuate its considerable charm.

Heritage hoteliers, the Neemrana Group, operate a compact 14-room hotel here. Set just back from the *promenade de plage*, it's housed in a French mansion that was built in 1789–90, but was substantially rebuilt in the late 19th century. From 1952 to the early '90s, it housed the administration offices of Pondicherry's Department of Education (hence the sign above the front door reading "Instruction Publique") until the roof literally fell in. It was then that Neemrana stepped in and literally stripped the building to its bare bones—and set about reconstructing it in a style sensitive to the elegant proportions of the original. From its blush pink neo-classical façade (the original color that was resurrected from beneath layers of whitewash) (*right*), to its spacious and individual rooms and shaded central courtyard (*below left*), the property exudes a style *sympathetique*.

This hotel's strength lies both in its atmosphere and in the details. Teak shutters and window frames were removed, stripped down to the wood, ironwork refitted (or if necessary re-fired as faithful copies of the originals) and returned to the large windows. Original lamp fittings and fans were retained wherever possible, while terracotta tiles were painstakingly repaired and replaced. High ceilings were left much as they were found, and today their exposed beams display a softly distressed shade of aquamarine.

In addition to these small, but crucial, touches is an eclectic array of colonial and hybrid furniture and art pieces sourced from within Pondicherry and around Tamil Nadu and Kerala. Set against a pale palette of white walls, they delight both in the public areas, such as in the large, airy first-floor gallery, or in the rooms themselves. Dowry chests double as luggage racks, planters' chairs beckon for an afternoon nap, four-posters signify a past era of romance and intrigue. Bed legs have been converted into bedside lamps, and air-conditioners are subtly concealed behind custom-made wooden chests.

One of the owners, Francis Wacziarg, is an avid collector of etchings *indiennes*, and these are displayed on every possible wall surface. Be they black-and-white portraits of colonials, Ravi Varma oleographs, kitsch colorful expressions of Hindu deities, aquarelles of southern India, or postcards once mailed out of Pondicherry to France and now returned, they encourage one to linger and to wonder. There is also a selection of old mirrors, and the restaurant, aptly named Carte Blanche, houses a selection of rare old maps that illustrate the Coromandel Coast as well as the French possessions through the decades.

Carte Blanche serves a melée of dishes that reflects the sense of place so inherent in the Hotel de l'Orient. It offers a creole cuisine that blends French techniques and dishes with spicy South Indian flavors. Leek tart, fresh chili squid salad, Chicken 65 (a local speciality) and mussels with coriander are just some examples of what to expect. Old silver cutlery and hand-crafted ceramic jugs add a homespun touch. Breakfast comprises fruit and pastries with homemade jams from the Neemrana kitchens—and steaming organic coffee.

Each of the suites and rooms is named after a former French *comptoir*, *loge* or *factoire*, and the dates of French occupation are marked on the doors. Every room has its own character, and size and amenities vary. Some of the more spacious have a private terrace or a large sitting area, while one is a tiny attic room accessible via a steep flight of stairs. Nostalgic appeal is created by the use of four-poster beds made up with soft Indian cotton sheets and *resais* (Indian duvets), Indian-made Savonnerie rugs, heavy wardrobes and French armoires.

Although the Hotel de l'Orient is certainly not five-star, or even four-star for that matter, it offers a luxurious experience nonetheless. Call it luxury redefined, if you will. The luxury of slowing down, stepping back a little in time, and soaking in the atmosphere of a quaint coastal town—one that captured the imagination of generations of French traders, and which has now been somewhat resurrected for the modern traveler in this delightful auberge.

17 Rue Romain Rolland, Pondicherry 605 001, Tamil Nadu, India
tel: +91 413 346589/3067/68   fax: +91 413 227829
email: orient1804@satyam.net.in   www.neemranahotels.com

The Park Hotel Chennai, India

The Park Hotel in Chennai, formerly Madras, is unquestionably the most modern hotel in India. With its cutting-edge interior design by Hirsch Bedner and Associates, Los Angeles, high-tech facilities and high-style service, it easily bears comparison with the new wave of "designer hotels" in the US and Europe. In fact, along with its sister in Bangalore, the Park has been accepted as a member of the Design Hotels portfolio (see www.designhotels.com). As such, it paves the way for a product still in its infancy in India: redefined hoteliering in the form of the cosmopolitan, uber-design, very contemporary urban hotel.

This is evident from the minute you drive up the circular ramp to the hotel entrance (left). A deep blue curved wall, punctuated with openings, keeps the hotel separate yet still connected to the city. On the other side is a stark lotus sculpture by artist Hemi Bawa. A huge door of beech and frosted glass swings open and you find yourself for one chilling moment in a small triangular space faced with another set of identical doors (right middle). This moment of disorientation only heightens the expectation—which is fully realized once you enter the multi-level atrium lobby.

This is, quite simply, breathtaking. Furnished in tones of olive, taupe and the palest aquamarine with chocolate carpet and pale cream limestone floors, the lobby is a lovely mélange of textures, surfaces, shadow and light. It is both restful and dramatic. Modernist materials—in the form of frosted glass, metal, transparent glass and crushed glass (all echoed in other places in the hotel)— are used alongside organics such as a large bamboo screen separating the functional check-in part of the lobby from the lounge area, sculptural flower arrangements, and wooden temple pillars doubling as occasional table legs. Leading off the lounge is an outdoor terrace with a metal, mirror and glass water feature that cleverly enlarges the area (right top). The flooring here is made from railway sleepers, a reminder that Chennai was a huge rail terminus, and indeed still is.

In fact, this sense of place is used to great effect throughout the hotel. Behind the check-out desk is a large panel of leather (Chennai has long been known as the city of leather) and the eponymous bar makes full use of the material. Separated from the lounge area by a DJ booth, it's a dark, masculine space, with dramatic lighting and only 32 seats; floors are of black leather and walls of suede. Black-clad bartenders with leather-studded belts and chrome cocktail shakers are sleek, slick and professional. This professionalism is carried through to the restaurants, conference center and each and every member of staff.

Sited on the premises of the erstwhile Gemini Film Studios, the Park Chennai toys with the city's movie heritage, translating it into a multi-media experience in all areas of the hotel. In the evenings the lobby transforms into a cinematic dreamscape—an interactive space of light and sound. Theatrical lighting changes the mood and snapshots of films are projected onto two huge white screens hanging down from the ceiling—today's echo of the movie-screenings of old. Music is a key element here: the hotel sound system is state-of-the-art, with meditative music playing in the morning, and gradually picking up tempo during the day. By sundown the lobby is rocking!

theleelabar

Similarly, there is a small video screen in each lift, and on reaching the residential floors, walls display some movie paraphernalia or other. The carpet is cleverly designed to mimic the count-down numbers shown at the beginning of a film, while old posters of Tamil film stars and black-and-white movie ads continue the cinematic theme into the rooms and suites. Each of these (there are 215 altogether) is suitably attired with beech floors, light wood workstations with fax, internet connection and anglepoise lamp and mini-bar cabinet with frosted glass doors. A quirky box made from recycled tetra packs contains a kettle, while the side tables are of glass. A curved false ceiling gives the rooms a softer feel, as does the fabric-covered bedhead and the double set of curtains—one of these sheer, duplicated between bathroom and bedroom, and the other, of heavier silk.

Dining options at the hotel are threefold. 601 (named after the address of the hotel), is the hotel's 24-hour restaurant. It has a buzzy atmosphere, with chefs strutting their stuff in the open-plan kitchen at all hours. There is a pasta station, wood tables with coconut shell inlay embedded in the shape of off-center mats and leather-upholstered seats with punctuated holes in the back of the chairs. For a more formal meal, try the Thai restaurant called The Lotus. Enter through a door that echoes the main entrance door and prepare to be ambushed by shades of gold and pink, floor-to-ceiling Thai silk curtains, a central gold lotus sculpture, seats upholstered in gold textured material, and two full-height lamps made with shimmering oyster shells. The food, as befits the setting, is sumptuous. The third dining venue is on the eighth-floor terrace, where night-time barbecues are held—and views over Chennai vie for prominence with the food.

When the hotel opened in 2002, the response to its sheer daring modernity was cautious at first, but very soon, the accolades started to pour in. "Chennai used to be far more conservative," asserts general manager, V V Giri, "but it has changed a lot. People are definitely more mobile and outward-looking nowadays." Giri continues: "Not necessarily do I say the Park Chennai is contem-porary West, more contemporary India. This," he gesticulates at the dramatic, sound-and-light show lobby, "is what India is today."

601 Anna Salai, Chennai 600 006
tel: +91 44 714 4000   fax: +91 44 714 4100
email: tpch@theparkhotels.com   www.theparkhotels.com

Cocoa Island South Malé Atoll, the Maldives

Mention the Metropolitan in London, or Parrot Cay in the Caribbean, and even the seriously cool drop their demeanors of studied nonchalance. Aesthetics and appearance—with a healthy dose of branding—are paramount in such worlds where the latest gadgets are as important as one's postal code. After all, anyone who is anyone chooses only Shrager-and-Starck urban resting holes, or the exclusive retreats of such groups as Como Hotels and Resorts. Cocoa Island, the third hotel from the design house of Christina Ong, falls into the latter category.

It is hardly surprising, therefore, that when the resort opened in 2003, the press descended in droves. Followed closely by European glitterati, paparazzi and even the odd celebrity, the hotel got the nod. After all, with interiors more Starck than shark (although there are plenty of the latter in the shallow lagoon) and the hip Ong Touch, how could they go wrong? Any hotel that has organic ginger beer pressé in the mini-bar gets the billing in my book any day.

Despite the hype, the atmosphere in the resort is surprisingly down-to-earth. I'd expected advertising types with phones glued to their ears, and designer-attired babes with champagne flutes and high-pitched laughs. But, happily, there is none of that. It's just your usual mix of bare-foot sun-searchers, diving aficionados and laid-back relax-and-rejuvenate regulars, taking in the calm, cool and beauty of island and lagoon.

Sure, they're doing it in an environment that is design-conscious and contemporary. Much of the architecture is by Cheong Yew Kuan (most well known for the Begawan Giri Estate in Bali) and represents an authentic regionality albeit with a modern twist. Rooms and suites are housed off an over-water crescent-shaped walkway in accommodations that echo the shape of local *dhoni* boats. With thatch roofs, dark wooden hulls and nautical blue-and-white paint finishes, they are creative craft. And crafted with distinctive details: upturned prows in blue, black and white; porthole windows; bulbous back sundecks with steps leading down into the clear Evian-water lagoon; and spacious, clean interiors with more than a touch of Scandinavian influence.

There are four categories of *dhoni* accommodation: two-bedroom, suite, loft and standard—and with only 36 rooms and suites in total, the resort is exclusive and intimate. Dark wood furniture from Indonesia, Sri Lanka and India, pristine white walls and vaulted ceilings are matched with light, air and lagoon views. Flowing, semi-transparent white embroidered drapes custom designed and made in India (with black-out curtains behind—a thoughtful touch) and a woven inner roof add some texture and softness, while bright dhurries and giant floor cushions in earth tones alleviate the restrained palette. A minor quibble is that the "boats" lie just a little too close to each other for total privacy, but when lit up at night, they take on a magical glow.

Bathrooms are clean-lined, with open-sided wardrobes and shelves and vented windows. Portholes, that from the outside look like windows, double as mirrors inside. A stand-alone oval tub, separate shower cubicle and stone-set vanity, are all cool and appealing. As are the bathrobes, made by specialist Italian company The Robe Works. Thumbs up to both the name as well as the double-layer soft cotton terry inside, and thin microfiber outside. Ditto the Shambhala bath products, which are produced by a UK aromatherapist from essential oils and therapeutic herbs, and are zesty, tangy and 100-percent pure.

Public facilities are set on the island itself, either at the sunset viewing side, or situated so as to greet the sunrise. The Shambhala Retreat, a series of open pavilions housing spa facilities, is in the latter category; particularly atmospheric is the wonderful open-sided yoga pavilion with sunrise views. A serious yoga practitioner, Mrs Ong first set up the Shambhala yoga center in 1998 in Singapore, and then exported her brand of therapeutic, holistic practices to the Turks & Caicos

very successfully. There is a short menu of massage therapies, body treatments and facials using natural ingredients such as salt, oat bran, yoghurt, aromatic spices and a variety of oils, as well as Ayurvedic treatments and the Renée Guinot combination of mild electric currents and fruit enzymes. Any Guinot fan will be pleased to see the latter in an area where treatments are often restricted to the Asian-inspired.

On the sunset side, where a sandspit conveniently creates an eye-catching apex, is a milky blue concrete-and-pebble-lined swimming pool, also shaped like a boat. On one side is an open-sided bar with a Toraja-style thatch roof, sleek furniture and a long diving-board table jutting out of one end. Directly adjacent is the restaurant, a slightly elevated, soaring open-plan space with hanging glass lights, plenty of room between the tables and an international menu based around the flavors of southern India and Sri Lanka. Particularly noteworthy is the almost total lack of landscaping on the island; for the most part it's been left as it was found. Hibiscus, sea grape and ylang-ylang scent the air as they did before the island was inhabited. It's a winning combination: artful naturalism or naturalist art? Your choice.

Makunufushi Island, South Malé Atoll, Republic of Maldives
tel: +960 441 818   fax: +960 441 919
email: sales@cocoaisland.como.bz   www.cocoaisland.como.bz

Soneva Fushi Resort and Spa Baa Atoll, the Maldives

"Ever Soneva so Speedy" was the name of the boat that sped us from seaplane past sandbank to Soneva Fushi; and "ever Soneva so special" was my summation of this back-to-nature (yet luxury) castaway island retreat. Situated on a privately owned 100-acre (40-hectare) island in the most distant atoll from the Maldivian capital of Malé, the resort is, literally and metaphorically, removed from the outside world.

You won't find Manolos and designer labels here. In fact, as soon as you step off the plane, your shoes are placed in a drawstring bag that reads "no news, no shoes" and you don't see them again until you leave. Barefoot and fancy-free sums up the ethos at Soneva Fushi; sarong-clad sun-seekers sway somnolently in hammocks, people cycle along jungle paths in shorts and t-shirts, and swimsuits, sunnies, beachbags and books are about all you'll need. That, plus a healthy desire to chill.

Yet, behind the rustic, back-to nature, jungle backdrop is an efficient, well-oiled machine. This comes in the form of more than 270 staff members, who maintain the illusion of the desert-island dream, yet ensure the creature comforts are there. In the tangerine-dream Soneva lounge at Malé Airport you can request CDs and movies from an extensive list; when you arrive at your villa they are already in the room. Behind the trees on the island itself are huge machine rooms that produce desalinated water, a satellite tower for telephone, internet and TV, vast tracts of vegetable garden that provide organic greens and herbs for your dinner, and a carpentry workshop. Your private guest relations officer communicates with base control by mobile phone; and high-speed boats and seaplanes are organized with iron efficiency.

But you, as the guest, need not deal with any of that. Far easier to buy into the dream. And that, indeed, is what you are there for. Soneva Fushi is a great counterfoil to its newer sister resort, Soneva Gili: there it is all blue and watery, here it is all green and jungly. There the sky is a constant presence, here it's only visible when you jump into the sea—and that's easily done, as all villas are situated in a private green alcove of mangrove and palm with a picture window cutting through to beach and sea. A network of sandy paths bordered by trees, greenery and shade connect the various parts of the island—and scooting around by bike is a lot of fun (especially at night!).

There are seven different categories of room, offering a range of choices for families, couples and individuals, but all are variations on the wood-and-wicker, rope-and-thatch theme. They are designed with a sense of humor and an eye for the unexpected: upper-floor walkways and open-to-the-elements balconies along with roped "bridges" give a jungle ambience; beds are huge and canopied; sitting rooms or seating nooks are characterized by a pile of tangerine, vermilion and orange cushions; and on every surface dappled shade and light play with textures and textiles. Indoor–outdoor bathrooms, the staple for tropical island bathing, have unbleached cotton towels, rope-ladders, sexy outdoor showers, walls trickling with water and huge tubs encased in dark wood. Some look like veritable jungle gyms. All rooms also have a private beach space, bordered by mangroves, palms and other tropical ornamentals. Here you have loungers, an umbrella if you need, your own dining table and chairs and large patios with overhangs and views out to sea.

Behind the rustic veneer, though, are a host of high-end gadgets. These you'd expect in the city, but on a desert island? No way. Nonetheless, they are there: CD players with Dolby sound hidden in wooden cabinets, TVs and VCD players delivered to your doorstep in a water hyacinth chest, and super-boiling hot, hot water. Each residence has a back door allowing access to the bathroom, so if you are sandy and salty from the sea, you can shower before entering your room. Nighttime turndown finds the bed strewn with rose petals. The folks back at base call these details "intelligent luxury": sensitive to the environment, without skimping on style and substance. "Ever so Soneva so sound" I say.

As with most islands in the Maldives, there is a sunset and a sunrise side, the latter being the most preferred. But what I liked best was the island's size. I felt that I had somewhere to go, places to explore, different things to see. On most Maldivian islands, you feel like you're more marooned on a giant sandbank than planted firmly on *terra firma*, but this is not the case at Soneva Fushi. Because of its size, Kunfunadhoo Island was utilized by the Maldivians as a farm island, and a bevy of chickens and rabbits wandering around attest to its past. It is also densely planted with a variety of vegetation including the indigenous *dhumburi* trees and salt-tolerant mangroves, further enhancing the landlocked legacy.

Soneva Fushi opened in 1996 with 25 villas. It now has 65 and some of the earlier residences have been recently refurbished with the addition of private plunge pools. The brainchild of British-born entrepreneur Sonu Shivdasani and his Swedish wife, Eva, the aim is to give guests "an experience" rather than "a product." In a back-to-nature setting, you're encouraged to chill out. Other amenities include an impressive wine cellar with over 300 vintages, the star-studded Me Dhuneye evening restaurant, day-trips to deserted islands, a relaxing spa, gym and tennis court, the general manager's weekly cocktail party on an offshore sandbank, outstanding diving and the care and attention lavished on us by our private guest relations person Saeed... Oh, and I forgot to mention—"ever Soneva so sunny" too.

Kunfunadhoo Island, Baa Atoll, Republic of Maldives
tel: +960 230 304   fax: +960 230 374
email: sonresa@sonevafushi.com.mv   www.sixsenses.com

Four Seasons Explorer North Malé Atoll, the Maldives

If the Maldivians don't have a couple of dozen different words for "sea" as the Eskimos have for "snow"—they should have. Amongst others, there's the transparent sea that allows you to view fish, white sand and coral as if it were right in front of the naked eye; there's the turquoise of the reef drop-off, a milky cerulean shade that indicates shallow water and a deeper cyan blue that tells you coral is below. And how about the slate grey streaked with white, where the wind has whipped up waves, and the sky is reflected in the ocean? Sometimes the sand seems blue too: just above the shoreline, it's a mirage of reflected sky. These are only a few of the shades that habitually hit the cornea during a stay in the Maldives; in reality, the list is endless.

No better place, then, to acquaint yourself with this pantone panorama than on board the Four Seasons Explorer, the first high-end vessel to ply the Maldives' outer atolls. Launched in 2002, the Australian-built, 39-meter (128-foot) 11-cabin catamaran was purpose-designed to complement the existing Four Seasons property in the North Malé Atoll and the new resort under construction in the Baa Atoll. From this fantastic, ultra-modern craft, you can take in any number of different seascapes and a great deal more to boot.

In retrospect, it is surprising that no-one had thought of the idea before. The Maldives sprawl across a generous 298 sq kilometers (115 sq miles) and comprise about 1,190 islands with 190-odd of them being inhabited and 70-plus of these islands housing hotels, yet most people jet into Malé International Airport, go straight to their resort island and don't budge for the duration of their stay. They may go on a dive or snorkeling trip or two, and perhaps have lunch on a deserted sandbank, but few visit any local islands and even fewer spend the night away from their resort. Yet there is so much to explore—and the obvious way to see it all is by boat.

In true Four Seasons style, this isn't just any boat. Interior designer Kat Kng who worked closely with the vessel's owners says: "The Island Explorer is no conventional boat. It's more like a floating resort, with ten spacious staterooms and one Explorer Suite. Built almost entirely from

lightweight aluminum so that it can cruise at 16 knots, each room had to be custom designed to ensure maximum usage of space." In keeping with its surroundings, the interiors are clean and modern. All rooms have eschewed portholes for huge windows that attract light and seascapes in equal measure. And there are no cramped bunkbeds: rather each room at water level has a king-size bed with signature Four Seasons mattress, a seating area with pull-out sofa and desk with amenities, while one deck higher in the penthouse at the prow, there is an additional dressing room, dining area and private sundeck. Wood veneer, beige custom-design carpet, white blinds and vegetable-dyed fabrics from John Robshaw are complemented by Italian Artemedi lights and modern fixtures and fittings.

While rooms utilize a restful green and beige palette, public spaces are done out in bolder colors. A teak upper deck with jacuzzi tub and springy metal-mesh loungers from French firm Hugonet is a popular place to watch the world go by. And there's also an internal bar and open-plan dining and lounge area where meals are served three times a day. Round-the-clock cabin service is offered, while the staff of 24 dispense drinks and canapés, take you diving, give fish talks and generally treat you like royalty. In fact, you won't be short of things to do. Ironically, an onshore visit to the Maldives would perhaps show the over-active twiddling their thumbs, whereas guests on the Island Explorer always have the next excursion to look forward to.

Three-, four- and seven-night cruise options are available and routes vary according to schedule. However, a typical shorter cruise would include diving at remote and untouched sites either in the morning or afternoon, a couple of beach barbecues, cocktails on a sandbank, sunset fishing, one

or two visits to local islands, such as a trip to Kaashidhoo where the remains of an ancient Buddhist temple dating back 16 centuries have been found, or a tour of a *dhoni*-making village, and pickup by seaplane. If relaxation is the order of your itinerary, take advantage of the spa therapist on board, or take time out with the resident marine biologist whose evening talks on the islands' endangered reef ecology are endlessly fascinating. Alternatively, if you are more out-doorsy, the Maldives are a sports lover's playground.

The choice is yours. As is usual with Four Seasons, the crew, from the Swedish chef to the ship's captain, is good-humored, knowledgeable and committed to guests' safety and enjoyment. They are also deeply committed to this piece of paradise they temporarily call home. Well aware that the islands are among the most threatened environments on earth, their aim is for you to enjoy them—while you still can.

Four Seasons Resort Maldives at Kuda Huraa, North Malé Atoll, Republic of Maldives
tel: +960 444 888   fax: +960 441 188
email: reservations.maldives@fourseasons.com   www.fourseasons.com/maldives

Soneva Gili Resort and Spa South Malé Atoll, the Maldives

If some hotels impress with the details, others blast you with the bigger picture. At Soneva Gili,
it's the latter: all wood and water, sea and sky—a panorama of driftwood-and-thatch clusters and
wooden walkways radiating out from the small island core. The seascape, horizon and sky is a
constant in the open pavilions, floating bar and watery spa; and the sounds of surf and roaring
wind comprise an entirely appropriate backdrop.

The resort has a cinematic quality not unlike a scene from Kevin Costner's *Waterworld*: rugged,
awesome and oceanic. But whereas Costner's film flopped, Soneva Gili soars. Set in a shallow
limpid lagoon, all residences are on stilts away from the main island. Some are only accessible by
boat. Also waterbound are the spa and bar, which doubles as a lunchtime restaurant. The only
structures on the island itself are the dive center, a (shallow) swimming pool, a couple of shops
and the main restaurant. Since the Maldives is primarily about the sea, swimming and underwater
life, this feels entirely right.

There are many other things the resort gets right too. Water bungalows are a heady hybrid
mix of rusticity and opulence. They are built in an architecturally somewhat shambolic style, with
pavilions piled on platforms, thatch roofs balancing on New Zealand cedar walls, semi-open
spaces leading down to the sea or up a circular staircase to a top deck. From afar, they look like
tottering tree-houses where bits have been added here and there over time. Instead of rising from
a verdant base, however, their bleached timber silhouettes are framed against an ever-changing
blue or grey sea and sky.

Inside, the bungalows are elegant and convivial. Instead of the usual sofas, there are two
lounging platforms in the open-fronted living room. Here, oversized handwoven cotton cushions
in the Soneva signature shades of hot tangerine, vermilion and Tuscan yellow work well with a
giant chess-set, backgammon table and hand-crafted distressed wood furniture. Ahead are a few
steps leading down to a lower deck with sun-loungers and access to the water. Cross-ventilation

is encouraged in the standard villa suites which is as it should be when you are out at sea. Off this central space are the bedroom, huge bathroom and a curved staircase that leads up to the upper-storey deck. If you prefer, you can sleep up top. The large comfortable day-bed can be pulled out from beneath its thatched protector and the equatorial stars become your nighttime ceiling.

The bedroom is generously proportioned with a large bed and seemingly free-floating mosquito net, accessories in wood, metal and leather, another seating nook and a desk giving sea views when the orange cotton cloth blinds are raised. A metal fishbone-shaped lampstand with natural shade is only one of the marine motifs; others include starfish doorknobs, wooden hooks in the shape of fish, a large leather box and anglepoise lamps with a bulbous leather base. Bathrooms are simply enormous, with glass-encased walk-in shower, walk-down sea bath, lovely his-and-hers vanities with beaten copper hanging lights, and a tub surrounded on three sides by a window with blinds. How you bathe is up to you.

In a curious reversal of the norm, the villa suites which are the cheapest (if such a word is applicable here!) are the nicest as everything, bar the bedroom, is open to the elements. The slightly larger residences and the stand-alone Crusoe villas have the addition of a not very useful kitchenette and wraparound glass shutters which one simply desires to throw open at every opportunity. Also, if you were to stay in one of the Crusoe residences, it may become just a bit annoying to always have to get into a boat each time you want to leave the room.

Much nicer to cycle, I felt. Each water bungalow is allocated an outsized tricycle and a bicycle, and the sense of freedom as you pedal across the water is exhilarating. Up and down the jetties,

room to island and back again, all the while the wind in your face and the sun on your back—an experience anybody would call pure bliss.

The *Tatler Travel Guide* in the UK awarded Soneva Gili "Hotel of the Year" out of the 101 best hotels in 2002 and it fully deserves the accolade. Besides the bicycles, other thoughtful touches include a stereo with quadraphonic sound, CDs and VCDs for loan from an extensive list, cloth covers on the bottom of wine glasses so condensation doesn't saturate your sarong, a "pillow menu" with therapeutic pillows for snorers, insomniacs and specialist sleepers, and a complimentary bottle of *méthode champagnoise* wine from the Soneva Vineyard in France. In addition, each villa is allocated a guest relations person who looks after you from arrival to departure, and is on hand 24 hours a day should you need him or her. Ours reiterated—twice, in fact—that we could telephone her at any time of day or night. This didn't prove to be necessary, however, as we were wonderfully looked after by each and every staff member. Our summing up? "Ever Soneva so Special" in a word. Sorry…four!

Lankanfushi Island, Malé Atoll, Republic of Maldives
tel: +960 440 304   fax: +960 440 305
email: sonresa@sonevagili.com.mv   www.sixsenses.com

Ulpotha   near Embogama, Sri Lanka

It's a still, clear Sri Lankan morning, and I'm sipping tea in a wattle-and-daub hut in what must be one of Sri Lanka's most peaceful pieces of countryside. A pan is boiling on a traditional mud range at one end, and huge bunches of bananas hang from the rafters. I'm cool from an early swim in the nearby tank (reservoir), where my only companions were butterflies, birds, a lugubrious buffalo and a giant monitor lizard—and the hills that ring it on one side and tiny paddy fields in every shade of pre-harvest yellow, copper and gold, on the other. I'm chatting to Mudyanse Tennekoon, one of the founders of this magical property. He is white-bearded, elderly, a little frail.

"When I was a boy, my father who was a farmer like everyone I knew, said he had found the perfect job for me—to become a liar. We argued back and forth about this… After all," and here indignation sprang from the old man's eyes as he reminisced, "I wanted to be an honorable man. But my father said that I should look to all the advocates, all the judges, all the proctors. They are all making lots of money, said my father. You, too, can be rich.

"Do you know what my reply was?" Here, Tennekoon paused, and seemed to lose the thread. I prompted him. "Oh yes," he resumed, "I said…I don't want to be a liar. I want to be a farmer."

And that is exactly what he is. But certainly not an ordinary farmer, and not in the manner that his father may have envisaged. Because Tennekoon, along with ex-UK estate agent Giles Scott and Colombo-based investment banker Viren Perera, is the owner of 24 acres (10 hectares) of land that comprises the Ulpotha Sanctuary—and is conducting a holistic, lifestyle experiment that many less assured than himself would certainly have shied away from.

Before the three partners acquired it, Ulpotha operated as a typical estate. At the center was the old manor house, also called the *walauwa*, and around it villagers worked the fields, relying on the patronage of the owner and the management of the communal tank. When the tank fell into disrepair and the supply of fresh water dwindled, the site was abandoned. Enter the three idealists in 1995, and everything grew organically—including the crops—from there.

"Our first job was to repair the tank," explained Giles, "We had to change a weir that was misdirecting water as a matter of priority. Then, in a thoroughly roundabout fashion, we started to revitalize the agriculture." The friends agreed to cultivate only with natural fertilizers, replant many of the indigenous natural hardwoods as well as fruit trees, re-build the *walauwa*, encourage the villagers to return—in essence restore the Ulpotha watershed back to life.

Yet for this enterprise to be self-sustaining, other sources of income had to be developed. Which is why I was there. During December to March and during the month of June, Ulpotha is open to paying visitors on a one-week or two-week only basis. The income generated from the all-inclusive fee you pay is plowed back into the sanctuary. There are yoga classes from some of the world's leading yoga teachers, Ayurvedic treatments, a variety of different massage therapies and, when I was there, evening tai chi lessons. There's the tank to swim in, wonderful walking trails to explore, two tree-houses to climb, excellent organic vegetarian food—and the daily rhythm of an unhurried, relaxed lifestyle in harmony with nature.

Accommodation is in open-sided adobe huts. Scattered over the site in individual clearings, each is a little different, but all have walls decorated with patterned swirls from natural ochre dyes. Their thatched roofs fall from a central finial like brushstrokes. Within each is a raised platform with mattress, traditional textiles and mosquito net, plenty of shelving, water that is replenished daily in clay urns and comfortable cushions for lounging. Paths connect the various parts of the estate, and if the land is not given to agriculture, it is planted with bright hibiscus, lantana and other scrub-like plants. There's no electricity or hot water, but the toilets are surprisingly sophisticated and the outdoor shower is the ultimate in open-to-the-sky garden bathing; at the turn of the tap, fresh cool spring water rushes over a piece of bamboo and cascades onto flagstones below.

Ulpotha is certainly not for everyone, but when I asked one guest, he wrote this impassioned assessment for me: "It is back to basics in a big way, with all the benefits of a, in a sense, highly organized but wonderfully unstructured lifestyle holiday. The beauty of the place is its simplicity, its timeless detachment from the outside world, an abundance of wildlife, the integration of the center with an organic environment, alternative healing and body work, the community that serves it and the utter relaxation it offers. It appeals across the demographic boundaries engendering a wonderful interaction between people from all walks, stripped down to their sarongs. It is undoubtedly different, probably unique. Trendy? Yes, in a sense. Contemporary? In a very retro-primal sort of way."

There—that's it in a nutshell. Oh…and the sarongs come free.

Galgamuwa Road, Embogama, Sri Lanka
email: info@ulpotha.com   www.ulpotha.com

Kandalama Hotel Dambulla, Sri Lanka

If architecture isn't merely about buildings and space, but about how these components make people feel, the Kandalama Hotel earns a double whammy in my book. Not only did I find the wildly dramatic configuration of spaces and blocks—set against a towering rockface that is facing a vast reservoir—gorgeous to look at, it made me feel exhilarated too. Standing on a terrace with infinity-edge pool and tank in front, and vertical lines and horizontal planes of concrete decorated with trailing tendrils of vines or sprouting cacti to the side, was a jaw-dropping experience. Strolling through the hotel at dusk brought on another atmosphere. Bats streamed through the walkways and water dripped over spotlit cascading crevices and rocks; I was forced to ponder over things that matter—infinity, nature, God.

If this sounds over the top, just trust me. Go there and see. Designed in the early 1990s by Sri Lanka's most famous architect, Geoffrey Bawa, the Kandalama was commissioned by Aitken Spence, one of Sri Lanka's largest hotel companies. They had an option on a site at the foot of King Kasyapa's rock citadel, Sigiriya. Bawa accepted the commission but suggested a site 15 kilometers (9 miles) to the south on a rocky formation above the ancient Kandalama tank. He felt the original site was too obvious; desiring a more mysterious atmosphere, he wanted somewhere in the jungle, but with views, somewhere that was at the heart of Sri Lanka—somewhere special.

To their credit, Aitken Spence went along with his ideas, but design and construction were dogged by controversy. There was opposition from environmentalists, local communities, monks; plans changed and were adapted, and construction only finished in 1994. However, it was worth the wait. Ironically, the hotel has since won numerous international awards both for the exemplary way it preserved its natural surroundings and reduced or eliminated pollution, as well as for its truly outstanding architecture. It is the only hotel in Asia to win the prestigious Green Globe 21 Certification. And of course it has brought employment to local people too, in the form of nature guides, hotel staff and drivers—and from the fall-off of having greater visitor numbers in the area.

In its final form, the 160-room hotel wraps around two sides of the rock. It's a strict and austere sequence of buildings with open-sided corridors; primary materials are concrete and stone with polished concrete or black Kadappa granite floors. Two wings are attached by a slim corridor that literally tunnels through the cliff face. The hotel mirrors the shape of the ridge, and is for the most part built on giant piles so water from the hills flows uninterrupted into the tank below. A flat roof and concrete frame complement the context, allowing the hotel to emerge from the site. Timber sun breakers bearing a screen of vegetation rest against the frame. During the construction process, changes to the existing topography were minimal and additional vegetation was planted afterward both on the flat roof and all around. From the other side of the tank the hotel is almost entirely obscured by jungle.

Geoffrey Bawa was an instinctual designer who always shied away from vocalizing about a design. However, in rare interviews he stressed the importance of context—the people, climate, site, tradition and history of an area. This is extremely evident in the design of the Kandalama, where a series of views (and framed views) are presented to the guest as he or she moves about the hotel. Similarly the minimal ethos of the architecture invites the landscape—rock, trees, plants and water—into the building itself, both on the open-air walkways and into the enclosed rooms. It is also evident on arrival: driving along a 10-kilometer (6-mile) driveway through forest and farm-land, snatched specks of hotel tantalize as they are almost indistinguishable from the landscape. Glimpses of greenery and grandeur, concrete and glass, reveal themselves in segments as you take the winding route up to the reception.

Both public spaces and rooms at the Kandalama are minimal and monochromatic, although playful touches alleviate the severity. Giant wooden elephant statues with massive carved wheels in the upstairs lounge were envisaged by Bawa as a giant's toys; as far as ornaments go, they are colossal, but their fanciful nature brings a touch of whimsy into an otherwise quite stark room. In the main dining room, wrought-iron trees decorate what could have been a rather bland buffet room; and polished concrete floors in the corridors are stenciled with leaf patterns.

Essentially though, it is the natural environment that takes center stage at the Kandalama. The through-flowing breezes and the ever-present sounds of nature—birdsong, the wind in the trees or the lapping of waves on the lake—bring the outside in, allowing nature to take pride of place. Even though the architecture is monumental (it is nearly one kilometer from one end of the hotel to the other), the scale is definitely human. A word of warning to note, however: the Kandalama is serious package-tour territory nowadays, and you may find the hotel overrun with noisy groups.

P.O Box 11, Dambulla, Sri Lanka
tel: +94 668 4100   fax: +94 668 4109
email: kandalama@aitkenspenceholidays.com   www.aitkenspenceholidays.com

The Elephant Corridor Sigiriya, Sri Lanka

Community development, employment for local villagers and a commitment to the environment are but some of the novel precepts behind the Elephant Corridor, an unusual all-villa boutique hotel that threw open its gates in 2004. Correction, there are no gates. Actually, there aren't any fences either. The 200-acre (81-hectare) site where the hotel is built is a totally open-plan affair. Border-less, the hotel pushes boundaries in other ways as well.

The area where the Elephant Corridor is situated constitutes the north–south route for Sri Lanka's remaining herds of wild elephants—hence the hotel's name. The spectacular surroundings are definitely the hotel's major strength, as are its isolation, peace and privacy. The extraordinary Sigiriya rock fortress and misty blue Kandalama hills form the backdrop, while up front are swathes of savannah and semi-landscaped parkland planted with indigenous trees and shrubs. Bicycle is the sensible mode of transport—or for the more energetic, hiking boots and a bottle of water. For lazy days, lounging by the deep blue main swimming pool situated quite a distance from the hotel itself is another attractive and secluded option.

You're just as likely to bump into a migrating elephant as you are a guest—or so the theory goes. Not in the hot season, you understand, as that is the time elephants head for the higher elevations. But in the cooler months, they'll come to one of the watering holes to drink or bathe, and as all suites are equipped with US army night-vision binoculars, you'll be able to see them close up. Ditto any of the many species of birds easily spotted from the numerous nature trails. The Elephant Corridor represents a new wave in Sri Lankan tourism, where the natural world and wildlife viewing is combined with five-star luxury. Facilities include the services of a resident naturalist, an Ayurvedic spa, sports equipment, as well as trips to Sigiriya and the Cultural Triangle sites.

"Our aim at the Elephant Corridor," says Mrs Susanne Filippin, the executive director of the company that owns the hotel, "was to place an all-suite, high-standard hotel in a wonderful site thereby enabling discerning travelers to see Sri Lanka's beauty, people and wildlife in a totally new

way." Eschewing the package tourist to target individual travelers is key, as is keeping the hotel small and exclusive. Architect Anton Jacob echoes her thoughts: "I wanted to realize the creative vision of the owners—it seemed right to build something with a strong sense of place, but somewhere totally luxurious."

When Jacob first visited the area, he was blown away by the vast, endless landscapes and the brooding presence of the Sigiriya rock. After extensive research into the history of the rock and the surrounding area, he came up with a design that has its roots in the vernacular traditions of central Sri Lanka, but borrows freely from more contemporary forms. Utilizing only a very small area of the ample site, he built a huge gateway with an elevated dining area as the main entrance and reception area, and clustered around it a variety of villas (*right*).

Jacob explains: "We elevated all the buildings for two reasons. The first was to deter elephant and other wildlife encroachment, and the second was to afford viewing of the savannah from a height. Just as it is works to watch a stage play from a tiered auditorium, so it does to view wildlife from above."

For the villas, Jacob took inspiration from the tents of soldiers; their conical forms and stone, mud, thatch and red tiles have a touch of the African-inspired about them, but are nonetheless anchored in Sri Lankan tradition. Painted a creamy ochre on the outside, they are elegant and roomy within. Utilizing a palette of cool, deep blue and exposed granite, they come in a variety of sizes and configurations. All, however, have a private terrace and plunge pool tiled in royal-blue (*left bottom*).

In keeping with the hotel's environmental ethos, all furniture was custom made in jakwood and teak from over 100-year-old plantation timbers salvaged from dilapidated houses earmarked for demolition. Not a single tree was felled. Stone was quarried from a granite mine in the central hills of Sri Lanka, and its cool texture helps keep the temperature down on hot days. If you want to simultaneously remain ensconced within your air-conditioned safari-style suite yet take in the outdoors, a huge picture window affords panoramic views. It's called returning to nature, but with all conveniences intact.

Kibissa, Sigiriya, Sri Lanka
tel: +94 66 223 1950-1/53-5   fax: +94 66 223 1952
email: hotel@elephantcorridor.com   www.elephantcorridor.com

The Tea Factory near Nuwara Eliya, Sri Lanka

After a trip to Sri Lanka's up country, tea jargon positively tumbles off the tongue. Phrases like "green leaf withering," "tea rolling," "orange pekoe," "silver tips" and "fannings" become as familiar as the intensely green, precipitous hills densely planted with *Camellia sinensis* bushes. Colorfully attired Tamil tea pickers trudge up scores of steps carved into the red earth; quaint colonial bungalows and corrugated iron tea factories rise out of the mist. The climate is always cool and often damp, making the area an attractive getaway for tea trail tourists keen to escape the heat and humidity of downtown Colombo. And if you aren't interested in Earl Grey or English Breakfast, you will be after a day or two.

Nuwara Eliya (pronounced "New-rellia") was, and to some extent still is, the epicenter of plantation life. Despite some rather jumbled add-ons, there are plenty of reminders that this was once the playground of the British Raj in Sri Lanka. Cargill's department store, a lake stocked with trout, gabled roofs, a pink-brick Victorian post office and the country's only horse-racing track resolutely cling on as time-warp trophies of the past. However, times have changed—albeit not very much. For example, the Hill Club, a baronial pile once the exclusive enclave of the British tea planters, today doles out temporary membership to any Tom, Dick or Harriet (women have only recently been allowed in!). This enables you to take tea, stay the night, play a game of billiards and, if you slip the ancient retainer a few rupees, he'll keep the wood fire burning during your visit. Similarly, overnighters at the antiquated Grand or the venerable St Andrew's hotels do not offer much more than they did a century ago. It wasn't for nothing that Sir Oliver Goonetilleke, appointed the first Ceylonese Governor-General after the country attained its independence, aptly described Nuwara Eliya as "a little bit of England."

If it's something a little less shabby and stuffy you require, drive on through Nuwara Eliya, round a series of switchbacks and up to a lonely plateau atop a misty mountain near the hamlet of Kandapola. Here you'll find the Tea Factory Hotel—an extraordinary 56-room hotel converted

from the now defunct Hethersett tea factory. At about 2,000 meters (6,800 feet) above sea level with 360-degree views all around, you'll feel on top of the world—literally.

From outside, the building looks exactly like any of the other tea factories you'll have passed—and probably taken a tour in. It's a corrugated iron-and-sheet-metal four-storey structure, with wooden window frames and an industrial chimney at the rear. It is only on entering the lobby that you begin to comprehend architect Nihal Bodhinayake's bold masterplan. What used to be the Drier Room is now a roof-to-basement atrium space topped with a pyramidal corrugated iron roof; there are enormous brass-capped withering fans above, the original power-engine below and iron girders, line shafts and pulleys all around. Floors of *jarrah* wood inset with brass tacks and hinges have replaced concrete floors, but give off a workman-like ruggedness, as does the open-shaft steel lift. Old black-and-white photographs of the Hethersett plantation and architectural plans of the 1930s factory adorn the walls. True to tradition, on arrival you are presented with a cup of tea, a warming, spicy concoction of tea leaves, sugar, cardamom, cinnamon, lime, mint and vanilla essence.

Further exploration reveals how a combination of skill and vision have transformed industrial heritage into industrial chic. The Goatfell, a bar in the old rolling room, is a combination of rattan and rolling rods, while its more loungy counterpart, the Hethersett, has transformed a packing room into a pub. The old sifting room is now the Kenmare, a restaurant where a huge copper tea dryer hangs overhead and the buffet counter is made from the plantation's tea chests, the name and insignia of the company emblazoned in black print. Dinner is buffet-style, as seems to be the

norm in such hotels in Sri Lanka, but the food is good and the atmosphere convivial. If you are wondering what that underground whooshing noise is, don't panic—it's only the old generator kick-starting into life for the evening.

The rooms are a little less successful. Numbering 57 in total, they are housed in the old green leaf-withering lofts, and although comfortable and clean, they're somewhat '50s in character. Try to secure one at the front if you can—the plantation views will more than make up for the room's slightly utilitarian character. Three of the rooms on the first floor have large balconies overlooking the surrounding fields of tea.

Not surprisingly, the hotel has been the recipient of numerous awards, most prestigiously the Royal Institute of Chartered Surveyors (RICS) Award for Building Conservation, and the UNESCO Asia Pacific Heritage Award for Culture Heritage Conservation. It's a stunning adaptive reuse project which moved the UNESCO judges to comment: "The project showcases the industrial heritage of the Ceylon hill country where tea factories are the predominant building type, and suggests how this legacy can be adapted to future uses. The respectful treatment of the exterior allowed the project to maintain its contextual integrity while bolder interior interventions allowed the building to assume its new role in the hospitality sector." Quite so indeed.

Kandapola, Nuwara Eliya, Sri Lanka
tel: +94 52 29600/04/05   fax: +94 52 29606
email: tfactory@slt.lk   www.aitkenspenceholidays.com

Taprobane Weligama Bay, Sri Lanka

Paul Bowles, the American author more associated with Tangier than Tangalle, wrote about his experience of living in Taprobane, the impossibly romantic house-on-an-islet off the southern coast of Sri Lanka, in the '50s. "I had always thought it would be a great pleasure to own an island and live on it," he said. "Consequently, in 1953, when I had the opportunity of buying the small island of Taprobane, I decided immediately on the purchase… The house, sheltered by high trees, was an ideal place to work. On the side of the island facing the shore there was the sound of breaking waves on the sand, while on the opposite side the waves crashed against the rocky cliffs. Those two contrasting sea sounds were very important to me; they provided an ever-present musical background to daily life. The climate was hot, but the principal room of the house was 9 meters (30 feet) high, and this encouraged the breeze to circulate."

The house also encouraged creativity, as Bowles was very productive during his sojourn on the island. Every day he woke up at 6 am and the majority of his richly descriptive book *The Spider's House* (1982) was written on Taprobane. He was always astonished by the beauty of the tropical garden and forest all around and clearly loved the open-to-the-elements house set in its midst. He writes that he could hardly bear to leave; it was only when his wife Jane had a stroke that he reluctantly packed his bags.

In many ways his life on the island was not dissimilar to that of the first owner and builder of the house, the slightly mysterious Maurice de Mauny Talvande (often called a count, although sadly the title was bogus). He describes his time on Taprobane as perfectly contented, the happiest years of his life, and it was there he wrote his own book *The Gardens of Taprobane* (1937). A botanist and landscape gardener, he conceived and created both house and garden in the early 1930s. He describes the planning process: "I lay awake through many sleepless nights, picturing in my mind the house of my dreams for such an island as Taprobane. Many days were spent drawing plans and elevations; almost as many in tearing them to pieces, until I had finally come to a decision…

The house, being a home for the tropics, had to be in tune with the East, in its style of architecture, its coloring, its dimensions, its proportions and internal dispositions, and the details of the carvings and moldings." Fortuitously, once it was finished, de Mauny Talvande wrote that the house "fulfilled my expectations, after many small alterations and embellishments."

Variously described by others as a "tropical folly," a "floating manse" and "a romantic retreat," to de Mauny Talvande Taprobane was the culmination of a dream. An elegant octagonal structure with a number of terraces and five bedrooms on three levels, it was designed to take in views on all sides; its elevation, aesthetic and architecture were intended as a complement to the garden. Half-Palladian, half-Dutch in style, it is breezy and balmy on a calm day, terrifying and tropical when the wind gets up. The sound of the surf is a constant, as is the other-worldly atmosphere—it's part temple to the winds, part home, part garden.

Scattered amongst family photographs and portraits of both first and present owners, are books and games, sand and seascapes, the flotsam and jetsam of past lives. There's a seemingly Moorish-influenced mural of a Kandyan dancer on one wall, and a variety of verandahs to choose from. Bedrooms are all individually furnished, and have en suite bathrooms. There are six resident members of staff and meals are tailored to your requirements, but expect spicy Sri Lankan curries, salads, fusion and Western dishes. You can swim in the cool blue infinity-edge pool (put in by the present owner) or wade across from the island to the beach at Weligama Bay. It's only possible to hire the island in its entirety, so Taprobane is ideal for house parties, (rich) honeymooners, and "get-away-from-it-all" folk in search of seclusion.

Its isolation contributes, in no small way, to Taprobane's allure. After all, who could resist the chance of living—albeit for only a few nights—on his own private island? Over the years it has hosted many a tropical dream-seeker including Peggy Guggenheim, Arthur C Clarke and Somerset Maugham amongst others. Clarke compared Taprobane to San Michele and in his trilogy *The Reefs of Taprobane* (1957) he wrote: "The scene was so peaceful and so completely relaxing, I managed to escape the tyranny of the typewriter…[it was] the place I learned to wear a sarong." A more recent owner was described in a local newspaper as "a Ruritanian playboy" and a "skilled sorcerer," but what he thought of the island is anyone's guess.

Today's owner is Hong Kong-based entrepreneur Geoffrey Dobbs, who says of his home-away-from-home: "The first time I saw Taprobane I was speechless and like those before me had to make it mine. To me, it's a mix between fantasy and theater, a living mirage…a place where I can ponder, enjoy the company of my friends and forget the frantic activities of the world."

Weligama Bay, Sri Lanka
email: sunhouse@sri.lanka.net
www.taprobaneisland.com

Kahanda Kanda near Galle, Sri Lanka

Yellow Moon Mountain (Kahanda Kanda) tea is grown at a small, low country tea estate that also doubles as a luxurious private holiday home. Set on a slight hill just 60 meters (200 feet) above sea level, this hideaway property is both working tea plantation and restful retreat. Comprising five double bedrooms in four free-standing villas, as well as dining and living pavilions, interconnecting lily ponds, a dark green polished cement swimming pool and a full complement of staff, Kahanda Kanda is serious house-party territory. It may only be rented out as a whole—but for a group, it is tranquil, secluded and luxurious.

George Cooper, the owner and designer of Kahanda Kanda, fell in love with the site on his first visit. He says, "I went to Sri Lanka in October 1999, primarily because my grandfather and great grandfather had been rubber and tea planters there between 1860 and 1920. It was on the fourth day of my first-ever visit that I was shown the site and on a compulsive whim, decided to buy the place. Mad Englishman and the like!" Cooper fully admits that he went in blind, but it has been a rewarding experience. "I adore the place, I have a great respect for Sri Lankans, who are utterly delightful, and I employ 15 people on the property including nine working on the plantation. With that comes a responsibility, which I take seriously, and I regard them as part of an extended family."

It is this relaxed family feel, as well as the beauty of the surroundings, that makes a visit to Kahanda Kanda so memorable. Mahenda, the estate manager, will happily take you on a tour of the estate, but if you prefer poolside relaxation or trips to Galle and the surrounding beaches, that is fine too. A staff of six look after everyone quite beautifully, from presenting a cool lime-based drink on arrival accompanied with a cold face towel to preparing exotic dinners. There is a menu book from which to choose what you wish to eat and the chef is well versed in Thai food and European fare as well as Sri Lankan and Indian cuisine. Staff will answer all needs: they take turns to do the food shopping, arrange transport for visits to sites of interest, take care of the laundry and are generally extremely welcoming.

Private villas are a popular holiday option in Sri Lanka. Many of the facilities normally found in a hotel are available, but guests also have total privacy. At Kahanda Kanda, architect Bruce Fell-Smith, an Australian based in Colombo, has created a mini-hotel feeling but with the compactness of a private house. The concept is a series of separate pavilions and aubergine-tinted cross walls linked by a slate-tiled walkway and bounded by a statement-making saffron-colored dividing wall that runs east to west across the center of the site. This central wall, the color taken from monks' robes, divides and separates the formal southern section of the house from the natural vegetation and bedroom pavilions to the north. Inserted slanted windows provide glimpses of the valley and jungle as one proceeds along the wall and "through" the house. At one end is a tall water tower.

There are eight brick-and-concrete buildings in total; each is rendered and painted white and roofed with original Sri Lankan tiles. The various buildings have either views over Koggala Lake to the south, or over a valley and jungle to the north. There is a strength and vitality to the complex that comes from the use of stone rubble foundation walls and the saffron and aubergine walls; but the use of water and plants softens the overall effect. "I believe the design represents a contemporary solution to a Sri Lankan-style building," says Fell-Smith, "but the separate pavilion approach is a breakaway from tradition."

Cooper custom designed much of the furniture himself. Eschewing the heavy colonial pieces so prevalent in Sri Lanka, he opted for a more modern look. Utilizing ebony, teak, jakwood, rattan and *kittul* wood, each piece is individually crafted with both sleek lines and comfort in mind. In the dining pavilion, a large table composed of two identical halves has a brushed stainless-steel cube at center and a teak top with ebony banding. Made by a craftsman in Bentota to Cooper's specifications, chairs are metal and coated in black leather. Net-draped four-posters in the suites are traditional in style, and bathrooms have outdoor showers.

"I wanted to create a home that is the antithesis to the way I live in England," explains Cooper. "There everything radiates from the inside; here it is all open-plan." To this end, water acts as a unifying element with carefully selected plants and choice water features giving the complex a sense of cool and quiet. And because the site is slightly elevated, there are cooling breezes and no need for air-conditioning. A rare combination in the tropics.

Angulugaha, Galle, Sri Lanka
tel: +94 91 22 36499
email: eden@villasinsrilanka.com   www.villasinsrilanka.com

The Sun House Galle, Sri Lanka

Galle is at the point of southwest Sri Lanka where the Bay of Bengal meets the Indian Ocean. It is an atmospheric town with a remarkable historical legacy that has captured the imagination of many. Its old section is a criss-cross grid of lanes, alleyways and ancient buildings all set within fortress confines; it's a great place to wander around. Originally occupied in the 16th century by the Portuguese, who built a small fort called Santa Cruz there, it was taken over in 1663 by the Dutch. The new rulers immediately set to work on another fortress, this time with gigantic ramparts and massive fortified walls. Built to house a city, it contains a fascinating network of circuitous lanes, shady squares and arches, both Anglican and Dutch churches and various buildings in various states of (dis)repair.

These buildings have proved remarkably robust, and are again attracting the attention of outsiders. Since peace talks in Sri Lanka gained momentum, Europeans (many from Hong Kong) have descended on the little town to buy both land and built heritage. In fact, Galle is experiencing a re-colonization of sorts, but this time it's fueled by the prospect of profits and lifestyle, rather than profits and power. In the first six months of 2003, 41 buildings within the fort were bought by expatriates; some intend to renovate and use them as holiday homes, some are opening restaurants, cafés and bars, others intend to live in them.

Only time will tell whether all this development will change Galle significantly—but whatever the outcome, the fort area is still a must-see. After an afternoon of sightseeing down there, take a short *tuk-tuk* ride past the fish market and up Richmond Hill to the long-established and well-run auberge known as the Sun House. You'll feel like you're going home. Because that's what the Sun House is. You're invited to treat this delightful, small hotel as you would a home: If you want to put on some music, choose a CD from the decent CD collection. If it's a quiet read you want, take something from one of the floor-to-ceiling bookcases. Select your spot, on a white lounger under the shady mango tree, on your own bit of balcony in front of your room (*right*), or down by the pool at the bottom of the plumeria-planted, terraced garden (*top left*). If you fancy a drink, there's always someone around to fix one for you— or just help yourself.

One of the reasons the Sun House seems more home than hotel is because it cannot accommodate many guests, having only five bedrooms and one suite. Another is that they are all under the one roof, within a wonderful, wide-porticoed colonial mansion built by a Scottish spice merchant in the 1860s. Before the present owner bought the house, it was extensively renovated by an American decorator who also added the suite of rooms at the back to house many of the guestrooms.

White is the predominant color at the Sun House. Stark and simple, walls are broken by wide doors with the original fretwork lintels above and louvered shuttered windows between, giving the impression that even when inside you may as well be out. Huge tropical flower arrangements, retro furniture, coffee-tables scattered with design magazines and enormous armoires contribute

to the colonial-chic homely feeling, while on any part of the wraparound verandah you are encouraged to put your feet up. Clearly the first owner was cognizant with more than just his cinnamon and nutmeg: he had an eye for location too. From any part of the house you get a wonderful vista over the old fortification of Galle and to the ocean beyond.

Resident manager, Henri Tatham, exudes bonhomie; she has that special gift of making each and every visitor feel welcome. As far as is possible she greets each new guest on arrival, and personally gives them her time and a tour of the facilities. It is as if she is the hostess of an intimate house-party, dispensing drinks and information in equal measure. "It is all very casual, very home-away-from-home," she explains. "We don't stand on ceremony here at all."

Having said that, there *is* a sense of ceremony come evening, when the sun sets over the Indian Ocean. Soirées at the Sun House are best described as glamorously understated. Glass-topped tables set for dinner in the breezy loggia and verandah are candlelit, covered with stylish linen and strewn with jasmine petals. Effective garden lighting outlines the twisted boughs of the frangipani trees on the descending terraces below, and the smells from the kitchen vie with those from tuberoses and other tropical plants. Jazz notes tinkle out from the living room, and ice clinks in glasses. Food is taken very seriously and the menu changes every evening depending on what the cook has found at the market that day. A la carte alternates with Sri Lankan curry evenings and barbecues, but expect to find aromatic soups, ocean-fresh fish, exotic tasting and smelling veggie dishes, and tropical fruit desserts.

On the night I stayed at the Sun House I discovered that the couple at the table adjacent to mine had gotten engaged that day. I wasn't surprised. Not at all. After all, it was the eve of St Valentine's Day…and the setting really was irresistibly romantic. All it needed now was for them to reserve the penthouse Cinnamon Suite for their honeymoon (*opposite top left*). Here, on either side of a blue-and-white airy space are two Belvedere windows; you can watch the sun rise over the jungle from one, and see it setting over the Indian Ocean from the other. It's clearly, absolutely, obviously the perfect place to fall in love!

18 Upper Dickson Road, Galle, Sri Lanka
tel: +94 91 438 0275   fax: +94 91 222 2624
email: sunhouse@sri.lanka.net   www.thesunhouse.com

The Dutch House   Galle, Sri Lanka

Fans of the Sun House (*see pages 222–227*) will be pleased to hear that the owner has opened
another hotel called the Dutch House across the road. Also known as the Doornberg, it is another
home-from-home hostelry—although more manor house than terraced house in both architecture
and amenities. It is also considerably more expensive and far more luxurious than its older sister.
Four suites are housed in a dappled cinnamon-colored mansion dating from 1712. Originally built
for an admiral in the Dutch East India Company, today it is a haven of calm and quiet, with a huge
expanse of lawn, a palm-fringed infinity-edge pool and elegant rooms.

Unlike their British colonial counterparts, the Dutch favored houses in which all the rooms were
interconnected on one floor. The early houses of the Dutch East Indies often had a central door-
way under a covered verandah or colonnade which led into a central square hallway, which had
front rooms opening on either side; behind these were the main living room or *achterhuis* and a
back verandah, courtyard or garden. The front portion of this particular Dutch House follows this
layout in every respect, but there is the later addition of a service wing on one side. More recently,
when it was acquired by the Sun House owner, it underwent a sensitive restoration and a third
wing was added to give the house a pleasing symmetry it previously lacked. It's now an angular
U-shape with central court fronted by a croquet lawn (*right*); on a lower level there is a swimming
pool wrapped around an old mango tree.

Channa Daswatte, well known as local legend Geoffrey Bawa's right-hand man (but now with
his own architectural practice in Colombo), oversaw the structural work. Great care was taken to
maintain authenticity. Roofs are steeply pitched with low overhanging eaves forming verandahs
on all sides. Tiled with the half-round clay tiles introduced to Sri Lanka by Arab traders centuries
earlier, they give shade and shelter as well as encourage the through-flow of air. Pillars are solid
and stately, and floors are made from polished concrete tiles, made on-site and inset with wood.
The vibe throughout the house is very feminine. Interiors were thoughtfully formulated by previous

manager Mary McIntyre and combine high-quality materials with comfort. Cool color schemes and flowing fabrics accentuate the high ceilings, and an atmosphere of calm and order prevails. Yet it is cosy too, with overflowing bookcases, Dutch prints on the walls, magazines on the coffee-table, and board games at hand. Dark wooden Dutch-style furniture was made in nearby Ambalangoda by local craftsmen; the owner wanted to replicate the best pieces of the period during which the house was built. Made from hardwoods—jakwood, ebony, satin and *nadun*—the pieces are hand-carved and sometimes caned to allow for free air-flow.

The four suites are exceptional in their sumptuousness and their size. Each is slightly different, but all feature four-posters draped in white gauze, cane-woven and cushioned settees, sturdy almirahs and cool tiled floors in mottled grey. Heavily swagged satin drapes in shades of gold and ochre are decidedly regal, while embroidered cottons, silk cushions and soft shadows add texture to the harder surfaces. An attached living room with comfy sofa, coffee-table, reading lamps and bookcase with an eclectic choice of books makes a strong case for the bijou boutique hotelier.

Bathrooms are creamy, pale and romantic (*opposite bottom right*): they exhibit the severe but simple lines of the cavernous bathrooms of the colonial era, but are softened with luxurious soft towels, modernist custom-crafted sinks, good water pressure showers and deep, fulfilling clawfoot tubs. Portraits of evocative nudes are by Sri Lankan artist Laki Senanayaki. Polished concrete and white ceramic cool, while the signature kitchen-cosmetic cinnamon scrub tingles the skin and fills the room with a spicy aroma. It's exotic and comforting, simultaneously.

A bit like the atmosphere in the hotel, if truth be told. Because the restoration has been so carefully controlled, the Dutch House combines the familiar with a slightly time-warped exoticism. You can recognize some qualities, but others seem almost other-worldly. After all, where else would you have the opportunity to sleep in a veritable hall (known as the Ballroom, *opposite top right*), the length and height of an average-sized house? Or potter around town in a 1930s vintage car, which, when not in use, is neatly parked outside the front door? It is the sort of place that ought to have a resident ghost, a pale colonial specter in calico, lace and linen, smiling beatifically while wafting from courtyard to colonnaded corridor.

The Dutch House has a no-children, no-television policy, so the house is always restful, cool and quiet. Breakfast and lunch are taken in the shade of the large water apple tree in the central court, while in the evenings guests are encouraged to pop across the road to join the house party at the Sun House. There's a full-sized croquet lawn (planted with special grass), an honor bar, and warm, efficient and very discreet service. Honeymooners, take note.

23 Upper Dickson Road, Galle, Sri Lanka
tel: +94 91 224 2730   fax: +94 91 222 2624
email: sunhouse@sri.lanka.net   www.thedutchhouse.com

The Villa Mahotti Walauwa   Bentota, Sri Lanka

About half a century ago, the author DJG Hennessy wrote: "To me the beauty of Ceylon lies not so much in its blue seas and golden beaches, its jungles and its mountain peaks, as in its ancient atmosphere. There is no nation, from Egypt of the Pharaohs to modern Britain, in whose literature this island has not at some time been mentioned by one or other of its many names—Lanka, Serendib, Taprobane, Cellao, Zellan, to recall a few. History lies buried in its sands, and ghosts of romance lurk among its bastioned rocks, for Lanka is very, very old."

If this appeals to you, and you want to learn more—or read more—get hold of a copy of Hennessy's *Green Aisles* (1949) and hole up at the Villa Mahotti Walauwa for a few days. It is the perfect place to relax and read in. With only 14 suites housed in a collection of colonial-style houses in a partially landscaped coconut grove, it is quiet, somnolent even, and very conducive to sarong-clad, hammock-hanging lounging. There is one of the golden beaches that Hennessy talks about to distract you if you want. There's also blue seas in front, jungles and mountains behind, but if I were you, I wouldn't feel too guilty about just staying put.

Privately owned, but managed by Ajai Zecha, son of Adrian Zecha the founder of world-famous Amanresorts, the Villa Mahotti Walauwa is run like a well-oiled machine. Service is unobtrusive, but it is there 24 hours a day if you want it. Discreet staff can arrange anything you need, from car hire to river trips to diving. The rooms aren't palatial, but they are cool and clean-lined, with handwoven fabrics, some choice pieces of furniture, antique fans and oodles of atmosphere. The restaurant serves fabulous Western and Sri Lankan dishes—the devilled fish is a must. The only low is that a train track runs along the bottom of the garden, between the coconut grove and the beach, and the noise of the trains can be a little disconcerting at first. However, you quickly get used to them.

It is clear that a great deal of care and thought to detail have gone into such a well-ordered environment. So it's no surprise to learn that Geoffrey Bawa had a hand—and quite a big hand actually—in designing the hotel. In the early 1980s Bawa had tried to get any number of friends

to buy the Villa Mahotti Walauwa, as he rightly saw that it could become a wonderful *hotel de charme*. When nobody would play ball, he eventually bought it himself—and spent many days working there, both with some of his younger team and alone.

In those days the grove was home to only one structure, a Dutch period manor house dating from the 1880s. It is the first building you see when you drive through the gates. Bawa left this relatively untouched, with the colonial carvings and wooden fretwork intact, and then proceeded to build on a number of other edifices. It suddenly became very clear to me as I wandered around the property that the sequencing of space, the creation of vistas, courtyards and walkways, the use of materials and the treatment of details was not merely some happy coincidence, but the result of intense scrutiny and planning. Each architectural element was arranged with a keen eye on the surrounding landscape, vegetation and views: light and shadow fell on certain choice walls at different times of the day; varying vistas were created by piercing picture windows in walls; and unexpected corners and private gardens revealed themselves over time.

In a rare interview, albeit talking about another building, Bawa explained his ethos: "For myself a building can only be understood by moving around and through it and by experiencing the modulation and feel of the spaces one moves through—from the outside into verandahs, then rooms, passages, courtyards—the view from the spaces into others, views through to the land-scape beyond, and from outside the building, views back through rooms into inner rooms and courts." This is particularly pertinent when viewing the Villa Mohotti Walauwa as an entity and endorses Egyptian architect Hassan Fathy's definition of architecture as "the space between the walls and not the walls themselves."

After a few days at the Villa Mahotti Walauwa, the "framed views" of Bawa's imagination start to become part of your overall experience as a hotel guest. Cinematic flashes of green, a glimpse of the sea through pandanus, even the momentary momentum of the Colombo–Galle train become enduring holiday snapshots.

Whether you're in your stark-white spacious room dreaming beneath a net-draped bed, bathing in an outside bathroom beneath the stars, or settling down for a cocktail on a cane-cool planter's chair on your own private verandah—there is always an unexpected view to take in. The element of surprise is the only constant. Go round a corner, up a narrow staircase, through a cool court—and look at something new.

Alternatively, you could simply head for a different hammock each day.

138/18 & 138/22 Galle Road, Bentota, Sri Lanka
tel: +94 344 287008   fax: +94 344 287007
email: reservations@thevilla.eureka.lk

Hotel List

India

Ananda—in the Himalayas
The Palace Estate, Narendra Nagar, Tehri Garhwal,
Uttaranchal 249 175, tel: +91 1378 227500, fax:
+91 1378 227550, email: anandaspa@vsnl.com,
www.anandaspa.com

The Casino Group of Hotels, Head Office
Willingdon Island, Cochin, Kerala 682003, tel: +91
484 266 8221, email: contactus@casinogroup.com,
www.casinogroup.com

The Brunton Boatyard
Fort Cochin Kerala 682 001, tel: +91 484 221
5461-65, fax: +91 484 221 5562, email:
brunton@vsnl.net, www.casinogroup.com

Coconut Lagoon
Kumarakom, Kerala, tel: +91 481 252 4491,
email: casino@vsnl.com, www.casinogroup.com

Devi Garh
Village Delwara, Tehsil Nathdwara, District
Rajsamand, Rajasthan, tel: +91 2953 289211/
94141 70211, fax: +91 2953 289357, email:
devigarh@deviresorts.com, www.deviresorts.com

Fort Tiracol Heritage Hotel
Tiracol, Pernem, Goa 403 524, tel: +91 2366
227631, email: nilaya@sancharnet.in

The Imperial
1 Janpath, New Delhi 110 001, tel: +91 11 2334
1234, fax: +91 11 2334 2255, email: luxury@
theimperialindia.com, www.theimperialindia.com

The Malabar House
1/268–9 Parade Rd, Fort Cochin 682 001, Kerala, tel:
+91 484 221 6666, fax: +91 484 221 7777, email:
info@malabarhouse.com, www.malabarhouse.com

The Manor
77 Friends Colony (West), New Delhi 110 065, tel:
+91 11 2692 5151, fax: +91 11 2692 2299, email:
manordel@ndf.vsnl.net.in, www.themanordelhi.com

Neemrana Hotels
A–58 Nizamuddin East, New Delhi 110 013, tel: +91
11 2435 6145/8962/5214, email: sales@neemrana-
hotels.com, www.neemranahotels.com

Hotel de l'Orient
17 Rue Romain Rolland, Pondicherry 605 001,
Tamil Nadu, tel: +91 413 346589/3067/68, fax:
+91 413 227829, email: orient1804@satyam.net.in,
www.neemranahotels.com

Neemrana Fort Palace
Village Neemrana, District Alwar 301 030,
Rajasthan, tel: +91 1494 46007, fax: +91 1494
46005, email: sales@neemranahotels.com,
www.neemranahotels.com

Verandah in the Forest
Barr House, Matheran 410 102, District Raigarh,
Maharashtra, tel: +91 2148 30296, email: sales@
neemranahotels.com, www.neemranahotels.com

Nilaya Hermitage
Arpora Bhati, Goa 403 518, tel: +91 832
276793/94, fax: +91 832 276792, email:
nilaya@sancharnet.in, www.nilayahermitage.com

Oberoi Hotels, Head Office
7 Sham Nath Marg, Delhi 110 054, tel: +91 11 2389
0505, www.oberoihotels.com

The Oberoi Amarvilas
Taj East Gate Rd, Taj Nagri Scheme, Agra 282 001,
tel: +91 562 231515, fax: +91 562 231516,
email: reservations@oberoi-amarvilas.com,
www.oberoihotels.com

The Oberoi Rajvilas
Goner Rd, Jaipur, Rajasthan 303 012, tel: +91 141
268 0101, fax: +91 141 268 0202, email: reserva-
tions@oberoi-rajvilas.com, www.oberoihotels.com

The Oberoi Udaivilas
Haridasji Ki Magri, Udaipur, Rajasthan 313 001,
tel: +91 294 243 3300, fax: +91 294 243 3200,
email: reservations@oberoi-udaivilas.com,
www.oberoihotels.com

The Oberoi Vanyavilas
Ranthambhore Rd, Sawai Madhopur, Rajasthan 322
001, tel: +91 7462 223999, fax: +91 7462 223988,
email: reservations@oberoi-vanyavilas.com,
www.oberoihotels.com

The Park Hotels, Head Office
Apeejay Surrendra Hotels, Pragati Bhawan, Jai Singh
Rd, New Delhi 110 001, www.apeejaygroup.com

The Park Hotel, Bangalore
14/7 Mahatma Gandhi Rd, Bangalore 560 042, tel:
+91 80 559 4666, fax: +91 80 559 4029, email:
tpbl@theparkhotels.com, www.theparkhotels.com

The Park Hotel, Chennai
601 Anna Salai, Chennai 600 006, tel: +91
44 714 4000, fax: +91 44 714 4100, email:
tpch@theparkhotels.com, www.theparkhotels.com

Park Hyatt Goa Resort and Spa
Arossim Beach, Cansaulim, South Goa 403 712, tel:
+91 832 272 1234, fax: +91 832 272 1235, email:
parkhyattgoa@hyattintl.com, www.hyatt

Pousada Tauma
Porba Vaddo Calangute, Bardez, Goa, tel:
+91 832 227 9061/62/63, fax: +91 832 227
9064, email: neville@pousada-tauma.com,
www.pousada-tauma.com

Samode Palace
Samode Haveli, Gangapole, Jaipur 302 002,
Rajasthan, telefax: +91 141 263 2407/1942/
1068/0943, fax: +91 141 263 1397/2370, email:
reservations@samode.com, www.samode.com

Shalimar Spice Garden Resort
Murikkady P O, Kumily-685 535, Idukki District,
Kerala, tel: +91 4869 222132/3232, fax: +91 4869
223022, email: shalimar_resort @vsnl.com or
shalimarresort@eth.net, www.shalimarkerala.com

Siolim House
Vaddy (opposite Vaddy Chapel), Siolim Bardez,
Goa 403 517, tel: +91 832 227 2138/941, fax:
+91 832 227 2323, email: info@siolimhouse.com,
www.siolimhouse.com

ITC Hotel Sonar Bangla Sheraton & Towers
1 JBS Halden Ave, Opp Science City, Kolkata 700
046, tel: +91 33 2345 4545, fax: +91 33 2345
4455, email: mail@welcomgroup.com,
www.welcomgroup.com

Head Office:
ITC Hotels, A-9, USO Road, Qutab Institutional
Area, New Delhi 110 067, www.welcomgroup.com

Republic of Maldives

Cocoa Island
Makunufushi, South Malé Atoll, tel: +960 441 818,
fax: +960 441 919, email: sales@cocoaisland.
como.bz, www.cocoaisland.como.bz

Four Seasons Explorer
Four Seasons Resort Maldives, Kuda Huraa, North
Malé Atoll, tel: +960 444 888, fax: +960 441 188,
email: reservations.maldives@fourseasons.com,
www.fourseasons.com/maldives

Soneva Fushi Resort and Spa
Kunfunadhoo Island, Baa Atoll, tel: +960 230 304, fax:
+960 230 374, email: sonresa@sonevafushi.com.mv,
www.sixsenses.com

Soneva Gili Resort and Spa
Lankanfushi Island, Malé Atoll, tel: +960 440 304, fax:
+960 440 305, email: sonresa@sonevagili.com.mv,
www.sixsenses.com

Malé Office:
2nd floor, 4/3 Faamudheyri Magu Malé,
tel: +960 32 6686

Head Office:
Six Senses Resorts and Spas
19/F Two Pacific Place, 142 Sukhumvit Rd,
Klongtoey Bangkok 10110, Thailand, tel: +66 2
631 9777, email: mail@sixsenses.com,
www.sixsenses.com

Sri Lanka

The Dutch House
(also known as the Doornberg)
23 Upper Dickson Rd, Galle, tel: +94 91 224
2730, fax: +94 91 222 2624, email:
sunhouse@sri.lanka.net, www.thedutchhouse.com

The Elephant Corridor
Kibissa, Sigiriya, Sri Lanka, tel: +94 66 223
1950-1/53-5, fax: +94 66 223 1952, email:
hotel@elephantcorridor.com,
www.elephantcorridor.com

The Sun House
18 Upper Dickson Rd, Galle,
tel: 94 91 438 0275, fax: +94 91 222
2624, email: sunhouse@sri.lanka.net,
www.thesunhouse.com

Taprobane Island
Weligama Bay, email: sunhouse@sri.lanka.net,
www.taprobaneisland.com

Aitken Spence Hotel Managements
315 Vauxhall St, Colombo 2, tel: +94 1 308
408, fax: +94 1 433755,
email: ashmres@aitkenspence.lk,
www.aitkenspenceholidays.com

Kandalama Hotel
P O Box 11, Dambulla, tel: +94 668 4100, fax:
+94 668 4109, email: kandalama@aitkenspence-
holidays.com, www.aitkenspenceholidays.com

The Tea Factory
Kandapola, Nuwara Eliya, tel: +94 52 29600/
04/05, fax: +94 52 29606, email: tfactory@slt.lk,
www.aitkenspenceholidays.com

Kahanda Kanda
Angulugaha, Galle,
tel: +94 91 22 36499,
email: eden@villasinsrilanka.com,
www.villasinsrilanka.com

The Villa Mohotti Walauwa
138/18 & 138/22 Galle Rd, Bentota,
tel: +94 344 287008, fax: +94 344 287007,
email: reservation@thevilla.eureka.lk

Ulpotha
Galgamuwa Rd, Embogama,
email: info@ulpotha.com,
www.ulpotha.com

Colombo address:
Flat 36, Galle Face Court 2,
Colombo 03,
tel: +94 1 386683

Acknowledgements

Both photographer and author are indebted to many people without whom it would have been impossible to produce this book. We would like to acknowledge the help, hospitality and patience of the following:

In particular, a very big thank you to Vikram Oberoi of Oberoi Group and Nazir & Catherine Rah, and everybody at Mountain Adventures.

Many thanks too, to Ashok Khanna, Deepika Bansal, Luisa Anderson and Caroline Dey of Ananda —in the Himalayas; Jose Dominic, Erine Louis, Mr P Subrahmanian of the Casino Group; Anupam Poddar and Rajnish Sabharwal of Devi Garh; Aruna Dhir, Pierre Jochem, Amol Kaushik, Aseem Pande and Sachin Pabreja of the Imperial; Joerg and Txuku Drechsel and Mr KP Francis of the Malabar House; Santosh Kumar and Francois Richli of the Manor; Aman Nath, Francis Wacziarg, Alok Kumar and Kulbushan Bhatt of Neemrana Hotels; Mr Oberoi, Vikram Oberoi, Ragini Chopra, Kavita Khanna, Anshul Kaul, Samantha Natraj, Sanjesh Jethi, Raj Rao, Nidhi Dabral, Devyani Puri, Karan Berry, Joseph Polito and Lincy Mary Isaac of Oberoi Hotels; Priya Paul, Priti Paul, Rupa Nair, Preeti Kumar, Lemuel Herbert, Mr V V Giri, Sumitha Gopal and Willi Wilson of Park Hotels; Claudia Derain and Hari Ajwani of Fort Tiracol and Nilaya Hermitage; Paul McNally and Karen Marshall of Park Hyatt Goa Resort & Spa; Neville Proença of Pousada Tauma; Yadavendra Singh of Samode Hotels; Maria Angela Fernhof and Noble Thomas of Shalimar Spice Garden Resort; Varun Sood of Siolim House; Sonia Bakhshi and Bulan Lahiri of ITC Hotels; Peter Wynne of the Taj Group; Geoffrey Dobbs and Henri Tatham of the Sun House; Mr UC Jayasinghe, Pradeep Dealwis and Frederick Melder of Aitken Spence Hotels; Ajai Zecha and Asanka Indusha of the Villa Mohotti Walauwa; Viren Perera, Giles Scott and Mudyanse Tennekoon of Ulpotha; Prasanna W Jayawardane and Mrs Susanne Filippin of Tropical Leisure Management; George Cooper of Kahanda Kanda; David Martens of Cocoa Island; Uday Rao, Carrian Sim and Armonado Kraenzlin of Four Seasons Hotels & Resorts; Bjorn Courage, Pierre Camorani and Charles Morris of Soneva Gili and Soneva Fushi; Ray Hall of Six Senses Resorts, Hotels & Spas; Kerry Hill of Kerry Hill Architects; Nozer Wadia of Nozer Wadia Associates; Cheong Yew Kuan of AREA; Bruce Fell-Smith; Anton Jacob; Pradeep Sachdeva of Pradeep Sachdeva Design Associates; Dr Subhodh Kerkar of Kerkar's Retreat; Eric and Christina Oey of Periplus Editions; Hardev Singh; Anil Kumar; Olivia Richli; Charlie Hulce; Jack Eden; Shanth Fernando; Jaya Imbrahim; Jet Airways; Peter Nielsen of Billetkontoret; Puk og Lone; Rajeev Sharma and Ambika Kurup of Patel India; Horst Dieter Ebert; Kevin, Tanis and Max McGrath; Tony Fernandes; Gillian Beal—and friends everywhere.

Published by Periplus Editions with editorial offices at 130 Joo Seng Road #06-01 Singapore 368357
tel (65) 6280 1330, fax (65) 6280 6290, email: inquiries@periplus.com.sg, website: www.periplus.com

Photos © 2004 Jacob Termansen (with the exception of page 194, courtesy of Ulpotha)
www.termansen.com
Text © 2004 Kim Inglis
Design by The Periplus Design Team
Book grid by Loretta Reilly

ISBN: 0-7946-0173-1
Printed in Singapore

Distributed by
North America, Latin America and Europe
Tuttle Publishing, 364 Innovation Drive,
North Clarendon, VT 05759-9436
tel: (802) 773 8930, fax: (802) 773 6993, email: info@tuttlepublishing.com

Japan
Tuttle Publishing, Yaekari Building, 3F
5-4-12 Osaki, Shinagawa-ku, Tokyo 141-0032
tel: (03) 5437 0171, fax: (03) 5437 0755, email: tuttle-sales@gol.com

Asia Pacific
Berkeley Books Pte Ltd
130 Joo Seng Road #06-01/03, Singapore 368357
tel (65) 6280 1330, fax (65) 6280 6290, email: inquiries@periplus.com.sg